4

PRAISE FOR *AMONG THE GIANTS*

"Great life lessons given out of an authentic journey. Jesse shares the keys every young person needs to chase their dreams."
—HEIDI KLUM, supermodel

"*Among the Giants* will inspire you to overcome the obstacles standing in your way."
—DOC SHAW, actor on *Tyler Perry's House of Payne*

"Although he's very skilled, what I admire most about Jesse is his determina-tion and heart when it comes to basketball. He embraces an underdog role which I can relate to on many levels when it comes to the game. This book will leave readers inspired and give a glimpse of a succeeding underdog's story who has encountered much but has just begun."
—GRAYSON "THE PROFESSOR" BOUCHER, And1 Streetball legend

"*Among the Giants* will inspire you to overcome your obstacles and excuses, plus help you master the skills needed for a meaningful future."
—JOSH SHIPP, Founder of Youth Speaker University

"Jesse is a great example of using what you love to do to make a difference in the lives of others. His enthusiastic approach to life is contagious and I am proud to call him one of my closest friends."
—TAYLOR GRAY, actor

"I met Jesse while filming the movie *Thunderstruck*, and we immediately 'clicked.' His passion for life and commitment to helping others has served as a great reminder to stay true to my passions. *Among the Giants* nails what young people need to hear!"

—MARK KREBS, former University of Kentucky basketball player, author, and speaker

"Jesse's story is one to be shared with anyone chasing a dream. *Among the Giants* is designed to show readers how to honor their passions and create a fulfilling lifestyle that makes a difference in the lives of others. He is doing just that."

—ELIZABETH STANTON, host of Fox's *Elizabeth Stanton's Great Big World*

AMONG THE
GIANTS

AMONG THE
GIANTS

HOW ONE
UNDERDOG
PURSUED HIS
DREAMS & YOU
CAN TOO!

JESSE
LEBEAU

AUTHOR'S NOTE

Dear Reader,

The giants I fought against in my life were not just the physical players in the game, but also the obstacles I had to face each time I slid my feet into a pair of gym shoes and walked out onto the court. My lack of height, lack of bulk, and seeming lack of intimidating presence all fueled the dismissive bias I routinely faced when the competition took their first look at me. How I met that challenge, how I drove myself with a determination fueled by a love for the game of basketball, and where that has all ultimately led me is what this book is about.

I hope *Among the Giants* encourages you to:

- Never give up on your dreams.
- Never let the odds stacked against you make you a quitter.
- Learn the lessons life gives you along the way.
- Look for new opportunities and avenues in which to "tweak" your dreams and create something that is fresh and uniquely yours!

As you read the pages of this book, take a new look at yourself. You may have to face different giants than the ones that I struggled with, but you can still overcome your obstacles, just as I did. My greatest hope for you as you read my story is that you will have a new energy and desire to pursue your dreams with everything that's in you. You, too, can create a life that you will love! When it's all said and done, you just might find, as I have, a bigger and better dream than you started with . . .

Good luck!

—Jesse

CONTENTS

FOREWORD

The majority of you don't know my name, although you've probably seen my face on television. At the age of twenty-four, I began starring in national commercials for Kobe Bryant and other NBA players. I've been featured by sports magazines and played in basketball games that were televised to a global audience. I've done interviews for radio, television, and websites. I've met and spent time with famous, wealthy, and influential people from all over the world, and I have relationships some of the most respected and intelligent business men and women in the country.

Do I think I'm special because of this? No. I know my efforts have been blessed! I also know that if there is anything special about me, it isn't necessarily my talent. It would more likely be my dogged tenacity to pursue a dream and my drive to put every ounce of my energy into making that dream happen! I was an underdog my whole life, but I refused to become a victim or a "less-than" in any endeavor I attempted. I always believed in myself, even when the odds were stacked against me. And they usually were.

Even with the success I've had so far, I still feel like I have room to grow before reaching my fullest potential. But I believe I am on the right track. The fact that all of this happened for me in such a short time is a true testament to the principles I have learned and applied to my life. I want to share my story and these "Life Lessons" with you . . . and I want this book to inspire you to find your passion and chase your dreams, so you can wake up every day and do whatever it is you love.

So let's get started!

Download a QR scanning app and scan the codes (like the one below) to watch videos for each chapter!

THANKS FOR CHECKING OUT MY BOOK. WATCH THIS VIDEO FROM ME!

PEP
TALK

WHY I WROTE
THIS BOOK

LESSONS AND DREAMS

hen I started writing this book, I didn't know exactly why I was doing it. I began putting my life's story on paper in Baton Rouge, Louisiana, while filming a Warner Brothers film with arguably one of the best basketball players in the world—Kevin Durant! I was excited about what was going on in my life, and writing it all down was a channel for me to record my somewhat unique experiences. Reflecting on all the lessons I've learned along the way, and acknowledging the deciding factors that went into shaping the life I am now living, gave me a sense of direction and satisfaction . . . so much so that I had an overwhelming desire to encourage others by sharing with them my journey up to this point. I've made many mistakes along the way, and it is my intent that you can learn from them just as I have. So many important life lessons can be taught through the experiences we have in sports, but unfortunately, many athletes fail to grasp the big picture. As a lover of sports and the writer of this book, it's my goal to help you see that big picture. I hope that through reading about my experiences, you will be able to make some of the same connections I did between sports and the most important game we'll ever play: life! I don't make any claims that these are original concepts, but hopefully you will find my story interesting and relatable, and be inspired to find your true purpose.

One dream and goal I had my whole life was to one day play college basketball and get my education paid for with a scholarship. Now, I was very small for my age, white (could I jump?!), and from a little island out in the middle of nowhere, so the odds were certainly stacked against me. But I had a dream, and I wasn't going to give up on it. To me, there was no other option. The lessons I learned along the way about myself and others still help and challenge me to this day. And I *did* play college ball, and I *did* get it paid for by scholarship!

You can start today and take the necessary action to get the life you've only imagined having!

What is your dream? Was it that you really want to do with your life? What is preventing you from making it happen? Are you worried about what other people will think? What they will say? I've had all kinds of people tell me what I'd never be able to do, and I've had a great time being able to prove them wrong. So can you!

LIFE LESSON #1: TWEAK YOUR DREAM SO IT FITS

Don't be afraid to tweak your dream. Growing up, I dreamed of playing college basketball on a full-ride scholarship and then going on to be a star NBA player. As I got a little older, I had to become realistic with myself and come to terms with the fact that I would never play in the NBA. I wasn't big enough, strong enough, fast enough, or just plain good enough to play at that level. I lacked the physicality it takes to be successful in the NBA. But that didn't mean I couldn't make my passion (basketball) a big part of my life and find a way to get paid for it; it just meant I had to be creative and think outside of the box!

I was blessed to be able to play college ball because I spent more hours than my peers perfecting my fundamentals and studying the ins and outs of the game. Although I felt I was good enough to play Division 1, I knew it would take several years to work my way into a starting position. I didn't want to do that. I chose to go to a smaller NAIA school where I could play right off the bat. This allowed me to be a starter and contributor from day one, and more importantly, get my schooling paid for. It was the best decision for me, and it worked out, although there were some trials and "characters" I faced along the way.

Knowing I wasn't going to the NBA after graduation or signing a big contract for overseas ball, I still felt there was another option. I wanted to try using my unique skill set with a basketball to audition for commercials and movies. It was a long shot, and I knew it. I passed up several safe, high-paying, and secure jobs (a tough decision), but in the end, I had to follow my heart and my passion . . . or else I knew I'd regret it. I encourage you to never pass up an opportunity to chase your dream! Sometimes achieving it may be just on the other side of fear.

I knew practically nothing about how the entertainment industry worked, especially for sports commercials, but I decided to go "all in" and learn everything I could in order to give myself the highest degree of success. I made a little sizzle reel on my iPhone to show some of my fancy tricks I could do and headed out to Hollywood, the city of dreams!

ALTHOUGH IT'S PAINFUL FOR ME TO WATCH, YOU CAN SEE MY EMBARRASSING VIDEO.

What I did know was that nobody was going to outwork me; I was going to give it 150 percent of my time and effort. This meant commitment to grueling, long hours in the gym and experiencing days of frustration and confusion about where this was all heading. But the outcome of my new choices were amazing. I discovered, once I got down the road a ways in this experience, that by tweaking my original dream (NBA/overseas playing), I not only kept basketball as a part of my everyday life, but I was also doing and experiencing things I had never even imagined I'd get the opportunity to do!

I never dreamed I would star in national ads on TV, be in movies, work with and become friends with some of the top athletes and celebrities in the world, be featured by magazines, and be seen all over the world on the opening day of the NBA playing ball with Justin Beiber! I could never have imagined that one day I would get to travel all over the world and make a living sharing my underdog story. I was just an undersized gym rat from a little island in Alaska.

By tweaking my dreams, I've gotten to do what I love on a daily basis and been more fulfilled than I probably would have been if I reached my original goal of being an NBA player.

Tweak your dream . . . make it fit *you*!

HERE'S A QUICK GLIMPSE AT SOME OF THE FUN THINGS TO COME.

LIFE LESSON #2: GO ALL IN!

HERE'S A FEW WORDS FROM ME TO YOU ABOUT THIS CHAPTER.

I love watching movies, and some of my favorites are the Christopher Nolan Batman Trilogy. There is one particular scene from the third movie, *The Dark Knight Rises*, which powerfully illustrates going all in. In this scene, Bruce Wayne is trapped deep underground in a prison of sorts. The only way out is to climb a steep rock wall and jump from a ledge over onto a rock platform. The distance was too great for any man to make, and falling into the deep chasm below would mean certain death. Bruce Wayne tied himself to a safety rope to protect himself against the fall and took the leap . . . unsuccessfully. He tried a second time, coming up short again, and fell down to the bottom of the pit in painful defeat. Each time, as he recovered from his injuries, he thought and strategized for hours about how he could get out of this prison.

Finally, it hit him.

The only way to make it out was to take a leap of faith. He knew his greatest chance for success was to abandon the safety rope and go all in. It was his only choice to escape. With that focused mindset, he took the leap that ultimately led him to his freedom. The rest is history.

Sometimes, going all in and taking that frightening leap is your best chance at achieving success! The fear of failing is often the biggest detriment to living your dreams.

As you review the lives of people who are ridiculously rich, famous, and successful, you will often see a theme. At some point in time, they made the decision to go all in, and they lived through some pretty tough times until they achieved their dreams and goals. Some lived out of their car for a while, some faced ridicule and public embarrassment, and many failed horribly on their first attempts. Included in that "club" are the likes of Walt Disney, Bill Gates, Oprah Winfrey, Harrison Ford, Stephen King, J. K. Rowling, Elvis Presley, Babe Ruth, and Michael Jordan, and the list goes on and on.

> ## "I ALWAYS WIN BECAUSE I'M NOT AFRAID TO FAIL."
>
> —UNKNOWN

I love to research and learn everything I can about the lives of successful people, and all of these people have, at some point in their journey, decided to go all in. There was no Plan B. They let their dreams, desires, goals, focus, and energy propel them forward. No roadblock or setback would change their course. They would accomplish their life's purpose or die trying. When you have that kind of vision, the world looks different to you! You find ways to use setbacks to change and improve on your vision. You work with your dream in clay instead of concrete. You work outside the box, looking for new ways to tweak things and get around the obstacles. Those obstacles just spur you on to new ways of thinking in order to accomplish your goals and dreams! In essence, the universe gets out of your way, and new doors of opportunity begin to open.

I have experienced this in my own life. In 2014, I decided to create a program that combined my passion for speaking and basketball to help inspire and encourage youth to make positive decisions. I dedicated myself to it and made the conscious decision that there was no Plan B. One way or another, I was going to make it happen. The more I began to take action—making calls, setting up meetings, enlarging my circle of contacts, and shaking the right hands—the more doors began to open for me in ways I never could have imagined! I've had major organizations and influential players wanting to partner with me and TV shows doing feature segments on me. The universe truly began to open up for me!

> ## "YOU'VE GOT TO JUMP OFF CLIFFS ALL THE TIME AND BUILD YOUR WINGS ON THE WAY DOWN."
>
> —RAY BRADBURY, AUTHOR

Still, I know that nothing has been handed to me. It has been relentless hard work on my part. No, it hasn't been easy, but nothing worth doing is going to be easy. The taste of success wouldn't be as sweet if it was easy to achieve! The sooner you can embrace the fact that you have to work hard to get what you want in life, the better. Take time to do your own research on those you admire who have done amazing things, and learn from them. See the sacrifices they made to get to where they are. Then decide for yourself how badly you want to work to get to your dreams! The choice is ultimately up to you. I, for one, feel blessed to live in a country that allows me the freedom to create the life I want to live. We have so much to be thankful for! What's stopping you from doing what you love?

Several of my closest friends are shining examples of "going all in." Nick

Huff is a young, successful entrepreneur who runs a website called *Hard Knock TV*. He interviews the top music artists in the world and has a huge online following and presence. He's involved in music the way he wants to be and has a great time doing it! Another guy who has gone all in is my friend Amir. Amir started Rosewood Creative. He connects brands with high level social media influencers and curates stories so the brands can advertise as organically and effectively as possible. He found a huge need in the marketplace, utilized his strengths and experience, and created something amazing. The part I left out of this story is that both of these friends of mine quit awesome jobs to start their own businesses. Nick left a job at Sony with benefits, a steady paycheck, and security to start up Hard Knock TV from scratch. Amir, at age twenty-four, left his position as the head of Nike marketing on the west coast to build his company from the ground up. They both had a reliable gig that many would kill to have. Yet they took a huge risk, and failure, statistically, was a high probability. Walking away from a sure thing takes a lot of guts. I respect them both for taking that Batman-esque leap and going for it. They've become the masters of their own destinies, and both are living a life they created for themselves. If you want to know more about Nick, follow him on Instagram and Twitter @ nickhuff, and to catch Nick's interviews with the biggest names in hip hop and for all the latest

> **"WHEREVER YOU ARE, BE ALL THERE."**
>
> —JIM ELLIOT, CHRISTIAN MISSIONARY AND MARTYR

news, you can subscribe to his YouTube Channel, HardKnockTV, and his website www.hardknock.tv

Looking beyond my circle of friends to even more recognizable celebrities, we can see even more examples of people who had to take the leap to achieve success. I love the story of Sylvester Stallone; it's incredible! Most of us are familiar with the Rocky movies and Stallone's success and fame, but not many people know about his life pre-stardom. So let's rewind to the beginning.

Stallone wanted to be an actor, and he put in the work taking acting classes and auditioning, but he didn't have any success. So he tried another idea. To increase his chances of landing a role, he started writing scripts that he could star in. He wrote relentlessly while living in a tiny apartment and continued to audition but was still unsuccessful booking any of the roles he auditioned for. Surprisingly, it didn't kill his spirit! He continued to write and hustle his manuscript, and eventually he got some people to believe in his screenplay, "Rocky."

Though the movie industry was interested in the script, they didn't want Stallone to play the part of Rocky. Instead, they wanted to use a big-name actor, and offered Stallone $25,000 to buy the rights to his screenplay. Stallone insisted he had to be the lead role in the film or he wouldn't sell. They countered with $100,000 for the rights, and were once again turned down. Next, it was $150,000, then $175,000, then $250,000! At the time, Stallone was riding around on public transportation and barely had any money to his name, but he wouldn't budge. He had taken the leap of faith, gone all in, and was going to see this through until he realized his dream and carved his destiny. Finally, they offered him over $325,000, but had to accept the fact that the only way that *Rocky* would be made was with Stallone attached to the lead. Since Stallone basically had no acting credits to his name, the producers didn't get a big budget to work with, but they still managed to get the job done. *Rocky* was the highest grossing movie of the year, bringing in over $100 million! It went on to win the Academy Award for "Best Picture" that year, and its tremendous success led to five sequels. Stallone became an instant celebrity and millionaire and had the ability to carve any deal he wanted in the industry as he continued to pursue his dreams. It would have been so much easier to quit and start a new career path, to just listen to all the people who told him he was being unrealistic and was wasting his time, but he didn't. We can learn a lot from Stallone about going all in, taking action, and not listening to haters. Every time I hear his story, I get fired up and want to wrestle life down to the ground and put it in a headlock. Don't quit. Don't make excuses. What's keeping you from going all in?

Another story I find very interesting is that of Robert Kiyosaki, the author of the New York Times Bestseller, *Rich Dad, Poor Dad*. The success from this and subsequent books have established him as a financial literacy guru who flies around the world in private jets and whose estate is valued in the millions. Though he is enjoying success now, Kyosaki wasn't always successful. After several years working for Xerox, he decided that he wanted to be an entrepreneur. He started his own company, but what many don't know is that at one point in his pursuit to be his own boss, he and his wife were actually living out of his car. They were broke and doing what they had to do to survive. But Kiyosaki embraced fearlessness. On the matter, he said,

"I'D BEEN WITHOUT MONEY THREE TIMES BEFORE THAT. I DON'T HAVE THE SAME FEAR MOST PEOPLE HAVE. I DON'T LIKE BEING OUT OF MONEY, BUT I'M NOT AFRAID OF IT. IT'S REALLY NOT THAT BAD. IT'S JUST UNCOMFORTABLE."

This fearlessness has become a success strategy for him. His persistence and unwillingness to fail, have led him to build an empire! His fifteen installments of the *Rich Dad, Poor Dad* book series currently have a combined sales of over twenty-six million copies worldwide! I've read many of his books, and they are phenomenal. (I'd highly recommend them to anyone wanting to take charge of their finances and create wealth.) Kiyosaki now has the world at his fingertips. His money and influence help millions of people, and he has access to influential people all over the planet. This is in stark contrast to the man living out of his car as recently as 1985. Not only did Kiyosaki go all in and take a leap of faith, he also didn't give up when he failed early on. We can all take something away from that. If a man can go from being homeless to being one of the most successful businessmen in our modern age, what's stopping you from getting to where you want to go in life? Be inspired!

Take the leap, and go all in.

4TH QUARTER

ME AND
KOBE BRYANT

THE REAL WORLD—LIFE AFTER SCHOOL

believe that basketball often provides us with a beautiful representation of life, which is a theme you will see repeatedly throughout this book. From years of watching and playing the game, I have seen firsthand that the 4th quarter is usually the most exciting. That's when I usually turn the channel and tune in to see how the game will end. Much like a basketball game, the "4th quarter" of my life has been the most fun to watch from the outside looking in, and that is the reason I have decided to start my story there. Once you see and understand my more recent years, I will rewind and share the journey I took to get here—the good, the bad, and the ugly—and then you will see how it prepared me for the fourth quarter and where I am today. So sit back and relax, and stop worrying that you missed a section; it's coming later on! For now, let's start with some recent events.

After graduating from college with a degree in Business and Marketing, I had some decisions to make about what direction I wanted my life to take. I remember being so nervous because I felt that whatever direction I chose, it was going to send me on a long path, so I wanted it to be the right one. I decided to leave my college town of San Diego, and head back up to commercial fish in Alaska. Now commercial fishing is no easy job. It is actually rated the deadliest job in the world, but the money is good! Making a good chunk of change—and buying some time to make my decision—seemed like the best course of action at that time.

FEELING LIKE I WAS IN AN EPISODE OF *THE DEADLIEST CATCH* WHILE COMMERCIAL FISHING IN ALASKA IN THE SUMMERTIME!

While on a commercial seine boat in Alaska, I had nothing but time to think. There's no cell phone reception, no TV, and you can be awake for periods of twenty hours or more at a time. The work is very repetitive, and you become robotic, performing the same task of setting the net out and pulling it in, over and over again.

For three months, I weighed what I felt were my three best options for the future. I could go overseas and play pro ball in Hungary, I could be a carpet salesman in California, or I could move to Hollywood and pursue a career in basketball commercials. I had some experience with auditioning for commercials during my senior year of college, but I still knew I'd have a huge learning curve if I decided to go in that direction. I weighed the pros and cons for each of these choices over and over again in my mind, trying to decide. I knew the safest option was to be a carpet salesman. I had an opportunity with a college friend to live in California and make $80,000 my first year out of college. That salary would have been more than comfortable, and it was a sure-thing. I was really tempted to go down that path, but something inside me told me I would be settling and taking the "easy" route if I did this. I listened to my heart. I didn't have any passion for sales, and although it was an amazing opportunity, I knew I wouldn't be happy with my life's direction when I came home at night. Basketball was still my passion, so I had to really look at my other two options. What would it be? Go to a foreign country where I didn't even know if they spoke English, or move to L.A. and see if I could break into an industry I knew virtually nothing about?

This decision was a real toss up for me, and I went back and forth on it almost hourly. On the one hand, I knew going to Hungary could be an exciting experience which I might never have the opportunity to do again. But thinking realistically, I also knew that the pay wouldn't be so great for a 5'8" white point guard . . . and that it would take me years to prove myself and earn a good salary. I also knew that it would be a lot of hard work and more years of pounding would definitely take a toll on my body, just as playing college ball had.

Then there was the Hollywood option. I barely knew anything about how the industry worked, but just the thought of it excited me! I was burnt out with organized basketball after some frustrating experiences during my last couple years of college, but a little fire started to reignite in me when I thought about making a living freelancing with my skills. I had gone to one audition earlier in the year, and they liked the way I was able to dribble a basketball and entertain them. Although there were many unknowns associated with taking this path, for some reason I had a certain peace about it. Foolish or not, I felt I had what it would take to carve out a niche in Hollywood. After speaking with my parents and receiving their encouragement (even though I'm pretty sure my dad thought I was crazy), I decided to go for it! I was going to choose the option that scared me the most! Before I knew it, I was on my way to Los Angeles to use my love of basketball to pursue a career in making commercials. I was willing to take a risk and chase after something I thought would be fulfilling. Once I made that decision, I was feeling pretty excited! Although I knew what I was attempting was taking a big risk and was pretty "out of the box," I recognized that I had rarely ever pursued anything in a traditional way before, so why not chase my dream and see where it would take me?

I moved in with a friend who had a place in the valley. This place was *ghetto*, but the rent was cheap! Since I didn't know when or where my paychecks were going to come from, I figured it best to live as frugally as possible. It was a tough adjustment at first. I had a great childhood home in Alaska and had lived in fairly upscale housing in San Diego while going to college, so this change was startling to say the least. I was now living in one of those areas around L.A. where all the billboards and signs are in another language and grown men just hung out on the sidewalks in the middle day, staring at you for no reason. It was very different surroundings than I was used to, but I got some experience playing the minority role, which was actually very enlightening for me.

As soon as I got settled in, I jumped right in with both feet and signed up for a commercial acting class right away. I needed to learn everything I could about what I had to do to start booking commercials. In the meantime, I had the inside scoop from friends on when and where the basketball auditions were, and I started going to them. One of the first ones I went to was a big spot for Champ Sports. They wanted a young-looking kid who could do trick shots. That was right up my alley! I felt like I was perfect for it, and they called my agent asking about me even before I came in. I was pumped and thought for sure I was going to book the job, especially after I did so well at the audition. I waited for the call . . . and it never came. I learned early on that no matter how perfect you are for a part or how well you do at an audition, you are going to hear a lot more nos than yeses. I didn't let it get me down because that's just the way of the game; it's marathon, not a sprint!

I went to a few more auditions and quickly learned that my fancy dribbling was a big hit! What I was able to do seemed to draw a big reaction from the casting directors who were picking athletes for the roles. It helped that I didn't look like I'd be able to do what I did, so there was a little bit of the "shock factor." There were a few times when I held back my performance, not sure if I should go all out, thinking it might be over the top. But each time I would mentally kick myself when I held back from just going for it. After leaving those auditions, I promised myself I would never hold back again. Instead, I decided to take it to a new level. If my fancy tricks were going to help me get noticed at auditions, I determined I was going to become the best "trickster" I could possibly be. I wanted to be able to go to an audition with the confidence that no one else could put on a better performance than me. I dedicated hours to practicing every day in the gym, focused on mastering moves I'd seen other people do . . . as well as inventing new ones. I spent night after night training in a nearby park by streetlights. I enjoyed it, even though I had to keep a sharp eye out, just to be safe in that rough neighborhood.

A few months into my time in L.A., a big opportunity came in the form of

HERE'S ME PRACTICING SOME MOVES AT MISSION BEACH IN SAN DIEGO.

a Kobe Bryant Footlocker commercial for the new Kobe VI shoe. I had been working hard, and I knew I was ready for this audition. Although I knew I had the skills they were looking for, I wasn't sure what "look" they had in mind. I knew the look was just as critical as the basketball skills. At the audition, I discovered the casting directors were looking for a high school–aged kid for this part . . . and that was good for me as I was often mistaken for being young-er. Unfortunately, I then found out they were looking for a black athlete for this particular role. I was a little disheartened; that was the one thing I knew I couldn't work on! At least I had nailed the audition, and I received a lot of "oohs" and "aahs" from the people who were watching. All I could do now was wait around patiently and pray for a callback.

I was in luck! My agent called me, and I was one of several athletes in the running for the role. I was one step closer to being in the commercial. I found out later that my dribbling routine had grabbed the eye of one of the casting directors. He told Footlocker that he knew they wanted a black athlete for the part, but there was one other person he wanted them to take a look at. As it turns out . . . I was that other person! I showed up to the final audition and was the only white basketball player going for the part. It was raining outside, so spectators were crowded into the gym. There were tons of little kids, and quite a few adults . . . all hoping to be extras in the commercial. I was called into a room with the director and had to run some lines and do some improv acting. It went pretty well, so then I was asked to play some two-on-two . . . as ad agency reps, the clients, and all the potential extras watched.

I don't know how else to explain what happened next. Some things are just meant to be! I had the audition of a lifetime; everything just clicked. I made all my shots. I dribbled through a defender's legs, looked back at him, and hit a no-look reverse lay-up. I stood on the ball and rubbed my defenders head . . . and the crowd grew louder with each trick I did! I ended the audition by standing on the ball, taking my shirt off while balancing, then throwing my shirt into the crowd as I flipped the ball up into my hands with my feet and hit a final shot. The people watching went nuts! They were yelling out things to me, like "Go, White Chocolate!" It went so well that the casting directors sent the rest of the athletes home before they had even auditioned. I felt excited about my performance; I knew I had done a great job! Next was the hard part, and so the waiting game began.

On the drive home, I got a call saying I was put on "avail," which meant I hadn't officially booked the job, but I needed to stay available just in case I was picked. The next five days of waiting were torture. I experienced every emotion that is humanly possible! On the fifth day, I got a call with the news I'd been wanting to hear so badly. I would be starring in a national commercial for Kobe Bryant's new shoe, the Kobe VI. Say what?! A small town kid from Alaska, who used to take a boat to get to school, would be seen on TV . . . all across the country . . . promoting a shoe for the best basketball player in the world?! To say I was excited would be an understatement. Although I spent Christmas alone that year due to the filming schedule, I was very happy and felt extremely blessed.

SEE THE COMMERCIAL HERE!

The shooting of that commercial was an amazing experience I'll never forget. I was so enthusiastic and wanted to do my best so badly that I would have jumped through a wall if they'd asked me to! I pulled two all-nighters during the filming, and performed all kinds of crazy stunts, from dunking on little kids, to jumping on tables, to chest bumping a grandma, to boxing and beating a professional boxer! It was unforgettable . . . and it went by *way* too fast.

The high didn't last long, though, because the day after shooting I was hit with the news that my grandfather had suffered a brain aneurism and was in the hospital. We were told he didn't have much longer to live. I flew out to Anchorage, Alaska, right after the filming to see my grandpa and be with the rest of my family. Seeing him in so much pain was the hardest thing I have ever experienced. He was one of the most energetic and strongest men I had ever known. The stroke had reduced him to a mere shell of himself. He seemed to be able to understand what we were saying, but when he tried to form words, only sounds came out, and I could see how much it frustrated him. Every night, my family would go home with a sadness and foreboding of what the next day would bring.

We were in the hospital when the Footlocker commercial first aired on TV. It's impossible to explain what it was like to see myself on TV all the way up in a little hospital in Alaska. My family went crazy, and everyone was so excited. It provided a little happiness for us during a very somber time, and I was thankful to God that he provided a little bright spot for my family and me. Even more touching was that grandpa got to the see the commercial before he passed away. It meant a lot to me that he got to see me do something like that before he left us. He always knew how much harder I had to work in sports because of my size. Even though he lacked the ability to tell me using words, as he watched me in the commercial, I could tell by the look in his eyes that he was proud of me. That was by far one of the most special moments in my life. My grandfather passed away shortly after that, and his death deeply changed the way I felt about many things in my life. I strive to follow the example he set with his life by helping others (he'd help out anybody who had a pulse) and living every day to the fullest. Very few could match the passion he had for living. He was an avid hunter and outdoorsman and was often heard saying with a mischievous twinkle in his eye, "Am I having too much fun?!" That attitude drew people to him in droves! His enthusiastic spirit is something I've tried to embody in my everyday life. It was hard to bounce back after my 'Gramps' passed. I was alone in L.A., and every time I saw my commercial on TV, it reminded me of him. I could see his eyes as they watched me run across the TV screen. In the end, I knew he would have wanted me to go on and pursue my dreams, so I pushed through the depression and sadness, knowing I could honor his legacy by living my life to the fullest.

"The harder I work, the luckier I seem to get" was the motto that seemed to embody my life. As I worked hard in my networking, daily basketball workouts, and dedication to improve my on camera skills, doors just started opening. And each door seemed more exciting than the last! I was asked to play in a Ball-Up game on national television against some of the best streetball

CHRISTMASTIME WITH GRAMPS, OR AS WE ALL CALLED HIM, "CAPTAIN ED."

players in the world. It went great, and I was even voted to play in the championship game as one of the MVP candidates.

One guy in particular who was fun to match up against was Grayson "The Professor" Boucher. I had watched him play on TV in high school, and people often compared me to him because we were both little guys with French names who could handle the basketball with a lot of style and flare.

Matt Barnes of the Lakers was my coach, and then NBA Hall-of-Famer

HERE'S A CLIP FROM THE BALL-UP GAME! (THEY NICKNAMED ME "SPIN CYCLE" BECAUSE SOME OF MY SIGNATURE MOVES INVOLVE A LOT OF SPINNING.) .

Dennis Rodman coached me in the championship game. Things like this didn't happen to people where I came from! I was from a little island in southeastern Alaska, and now I was on TV all over the world, brushing shoulders

MY FRIEND, MENTOR, AND STREETBALL LEGEND, GRAYSON "THE PROFESSOR" BOUCHER

with the famous people I used to watch growing up! I even got the chance to have *SLAM* Magazine do a feature article about me on their website. To be in *SLAM* was a lifelong dream come true for me. I had always read all of their magazines and imagined what it would be like to have them write about me. For it to actually happen was unreal. Let's just say I was pretty excited that I wasn't slinging carpet in Orange County or hauling gear on a fishing boat in Alaska! I was chasing after a dream, and with each small victory, I was gaining confidence and believing I could achieve even more!

The fun didn't stop there. Next, I got signed by a major up-and-coming

CHECK OUT THE *SLAM* ARTICLE HERE.

WATCHING THE GAME WHILE MY COACH, DENNIS RODMAN, LOOKS ON

sports accessory company called Deuce Brand. They featured me on their website, along other pro athletes like the Buffalo Bills' running back, Stevie Johnson. Money was tight during this time, but my enthusiasm pushed me forward, and somehow I seemed to skate by. I felt that my life had a purpose and a plan that was bigger than me. I continue to help other people along in their journey,

BALL-UP STREETBALL GAME WITH MY COACH, CHAUNCEY BILLUPS

and one day, as I was reflecting on all the amazing things God had blessed me with, a personal mission statement popped into my head. I knew I needed:

"TO USE MY LIFE EXPERIENCES TO INSPIRE AND ENCOURAGE OTHERS TO REACH THEIR FULLEST POTENTIAL."

As more commercial opportunities began opening up for me, I slowly developed a small platform where I could encourage others to chase their own dreams. For them, seeing an undersized, small-town kid getting to do the things I was doing inspired them, and that motivated me to reach the highest levels of success I could in order to increase my platform. I loved the feeling of having a positive influence on others, so I decided to try to reach as many people as I possibly could. I began to do this by embracing my fear of public speaking. I started sharing my message as a paid speaker, which has been truly rewarding and fulfilling.

It would have been much easier to have a stable nine-to-five job and be able to count on a steady paycheck and consistent schedule. But that wasn't the path I was on, nor was it what I felt called to do. I was on the path less chosen. I believed that God had His hand on me, and I was following His lead. (Who knew it would be so much work?!) I found that the more I submitted to Him, the more amazing doors He continued to open for me.

KICKING IT WITH CELTICS' RAJON RONDO WHILE SHOOTING A NIKE COMMERCIAL

My next big break was a second Footlocker commercial. (Gotta love those guys!) I got to work with director Antoine Fuqua and also NBA player Rajon Rondo. New York Knick Amare Stoudamire and L.A. Clipper Blake Griffin were also in the commercial, but unfortunately they weren't in my scene. I did get to spend some time with Blake at a Dodger game, though. My old college trainer is now Blake's trainer, so he invited me and a few other friends up to his suite to watch the game, which was really fun.

Things were starting to flow for me. I mean, here I was getting face time with an NBA dunk champion . . . most people would kill for that! I continued to feel blessed and tried not to take anything for granted.

I was now getting press in several major Alaskan newspapers and doing

YOU CAN WATCH "THE EDUCATORS 2" COMMERCIAL HERE.

interviews over the phone on the TV news stations. It was all new and exciting, and with each new achievement, I gained a wider perspective, and I began to look ahead to my next big goal.

To see the slow and steady progression as things started to come along for me in the media and press, you can visit http://www.jesselebeau.com/in-the-press/

I went home to Alaska for a month's vacation to spend time with my family, do some sports fishing, and also put on a basketball camp for the kids in my community. I knew most of them had seen me on TV, so I wanted to be able to give back in my own small town. I was hoping to inspire them to believe in themselves and take steps in the direction of their dreams. I wanted them to learn, as I had, that they were capable of doing anything they put their minds to—if they were willing to put in the effort it would take. The camp went great, and I got lots of positive feedback from the kids and their parents. I stayed in town long enough to volunteer time at two other basketball camps, and I really enjoyed meeting the up-and-coming players and helping them improve their game.

Money was still tight, and the sensible thing would have been taking on more part-time work. I wrestled with my priorities, and I decided that if I was going to be true to my mission statement, I needed to be helping young people now, while I was still in the beginning and "struggling" stage of my journey. I couldn't just tell myself that I would start giving back when I had made it "big"; it had to be part of my life *right now*. I wanted to be living my mission statement, not just tacking it on the back end of a successful life. It needed to be who I was and what I was about, starting today, and part of every tomorrow . . . whether I was rich or poor, successful or struggling.

We are taught when we are kids that if we give of ourselves with a good heart, sometimes we receive back when we least expect it. This was the case for me!

I like to call it a "God wink." I got a call, completely unexpected and out of the blue. The sports casting director who was pretty much single-handedly responsible for choosing me for all the major commercials I'd been in, wanted me to try out as a stunt performer for one of the lead actors in a new Warner Brothers film. I was dumbfounded. He told me I needed to go over to the Warner Brothers lot and meet the director who had done movies like *Malibu's Most Wanted* and *Big Momma's House 2*. I was excited but not too nervous. I knew I had practiced my basketball audition moves enough times that I could nail it on the spot. I was prepared, and my dedication to practicing gave me the confidence I needed in this situation. I met the director, John Whitesell, and he took me out to the court they had on their lot. Apparently it was built so George Clooney could play ball whenever he wanted to! The audition went great. I did the things he wanted, and he liked what he saw. "We'll see you next week in Baton Rouge," he told me. We parted ways, and I headed for my car.

This was another surreal moment for me, and it was a big step in the journey to where basketball was taking me. I was going to be in a Warner Brothers movie, and it was starring one of the best basketball players on the planet: Kevin Durant! I couldn't be more thrilled at the news. Warner Brothers flew me out to Baton Rouge, Louisiana, first class and had a driver pick me up and take me to my hotel. A rental car was delivered for me, and I was feeling pretty big time and excited! I greeted everyone I met with enthusiasm, and I was intrigued by the whole movie-making process.

My experience in Baton Rouge was one of those once-in-a-lifetime things. I became incredibly close with the people in the cast and formed life-long friendships. I got to spend time around and with Kevin Durant, and I even got to play ball and beat on him a little bit (staged of course).

I respected KD before meeting him and was pleased to find that the things I believed prior to meeting him were true. He was a humble, first-class character. I found him to be just like your average twenty-two-year-old kid. He likes music, video games, and eating hot wings (who doesn't?!). Yet, he was able to handle super-stardom and remain a quality person, which really impressed me.

At one point while shooting the movie, Durant left to do a commercial in L.A. A few of my friends happened to be in the commercial with him, and they asked about me and how the movie shoot was going. He told them "Jesse's got game; he can really play!" When my friends

SHOOTING "THUNDERSTRUCK" WITH NBA SCORING CHAMP, KEVIN DURANT AND MY BEST FRIEND, TAYLOR GRAY!

told me what KD had said, I was ecstatic. What was going on? One of the top players in the world knew who I was and thought I "had game"? How was this happening? Somebody needed to pinch me because this had to be a dream!

The rest of my experience shooting the movie went great. I displayed some of my skills in the movie, and I also got to jump off ramps and over cars and throw down all kinds of different dunks—from the safety of my harness, of course. Jim Belushi had to guard me in one scene, and I got to dribble the ball between his legs and make him fall over! It was a blast, and I will never forget any of the experiences I had or the people I met while I was there.

The big downfall of movies, I learned that trip, was craft services. There was a lot of sitting around and waiting all day, and you could easily get bored. The craft services people's job was to bring the most delicious-tasting food imaginable around set and tempt you with it, and they are good at their jobs! I ate.

And ate. And ate. I put on weight for the first time in my life, and it was not pretty! The joke around set was that I was going to become Jim Belusi's stunt double by the end of the shoot. For those of you who don't know what Belushi looks like, just know it's not the look I am going for! Other than my waistline, the experience was a blast.

After shooting *Thunderstruck*, I had the opportunity to join SAG (the

TAKE A LOOK AT ME BEHIND THE SCENES JUMPING OVER CARS AND HITTING SHOTS ON KEVIN DURANT!

Screen Actors Guild). SAG considers basketball a "special talent." This catapulted me into the SAG organization, a union that many actors take years to gain access to. This was just another amazing door of opportunity which basketball opened for me.

When I got back to L.A., I quickly booked an Adidas commercial starring NBA players Dwight Howard and Eric Gordon, and also rapper Big Sean. I did my usual thing handling the ball and again was thankful for yet another amazing opportunity. In my short time on this earth, I am learning to enjoy each day and embrace the journey each step of the way—whether it's tough or tougher, in the good times and the bad, when things are clicking for me

GETTING A LITTLE INSTRUCTION FROM THE DIRECTOR OF *TRAINING DAY*, ANTOINE FUQUA!

and when they aren't. At the end of the day, it's a blessing just to be alive, to be healthy, and to be able to love others. Enjoy it all, and be thankful! You'll never get this time of your life back . . . so don't be afraid to seize the day!

YOU CAN CHECK ME OUT WITH BIG SEAN AND DWIGHT HOWARD HERE.

LIFE LESSON #3: TAKE ACTION! EVERYDAY I'M HUSTLING, HUSTLING!

CHECK OUT THIS VIDEO TO HEAR SOME OF MY THOUGHTS ON TAKING ACTION.

f you're waiting around for your perfect opportunity or job to appear out of thin air, all I can tell you is . . . good luck. Those who have done anything of importance in the world have taken a leap of faith—maybe even a couple of leaps. You can't let your fear of not making it paralyze you into inaction. I've heard it said, "A person's biggest asset is not knowing what it is they can't do!" Nearly everything in your world is created by what you think—or not created when you don't think. Start thinking! Take action! Put some irons in the fire!

When I first found out about the urban-style watch company Deuce Brand, I immediately saw a golden opportunity to team up with what had the potential to be a powerhouse company. I also saw the opportunity to develop a beautiful relationship in which I could use their brand

> **"THE HARDER I WORK, THE LUCKIER I GET!"**
>
> —TED NUGENT, FAMILY FRIEND AND ROCK STAR

to market my career while promoting for their company at the same time. I discovered that Deuce was on the cusp of closing a deal to be the youngest company ever to receive an NBA license for their product. This could propel them into becoming a worldwide force. They were a young company, but I saw their potential, and I wanted to be a part of a brand that could someday rival the likes of Nike and Under Armour. I felt that I could contribute to their growth, and I wasn't going to sit around and wait for them to hire me. I started working for them and they didn't even know it. Before they knew what hit them, I was bringing in purchase orders, giving NBA players sample watches, and marketing the company in everything that I did.

Taking action worked! I didn't wait to be offered a job. I saw a company I wanted to be involved with, and I immediately got to work. It's exciting to be

> **"I NEVER WORRY ABOUT ACTION, BUT ONLY INACTION."**
>
> —WINSTON CHURCHILL, FORMER BRITISH PRIME MINISTER

able to be doing business with a company that allows me to work with pro athletes in numerous sports—definitely something I'm loving! Deuce has an amazing product, so I'm excited to be pushing the envelope and helping them grow. I have also been able to promote my acting, speaking, and streetball career as a by-product of this involvement. Through their channels and connections, I have made amazing contacts with other athletes and business people. My involvement with Deuce has been a win-win situation for both of us!

I got busy in other areas as well. Determined to be as successful as I could from a business standpoint, I did research to find and learn from people and groups who were smarter and more successful than me. I found a group called "The Entrepreneur's Organization." It has a network of over 7000 entrepreneurs spanning across the globe, most of whom were about forty years old and making around 16 million dollars a year. I knew I didn't meet the qualifications to join this prestigious group, but I was thirsty for the knowledge they had, and I was dead set on finding a way to make it happen. I wrote to one of the ladies in charge and told her my story. I included my Kobe commercial and the article from *SLAM* Magazine (online), and said I was willing to volunteer my time in any way they needed. To my delight, she wrote me back and said they could use someone like me, and we ended up having lunch together. And just like that, I was in!

I put together their electronic newsletter every week and sent it out to their members. It honestly didn't take long at all. In return, I was allowed to go to their events and conferences, so not only did I get to network with the millionaire members, but I was also able to listen to some of the top speakers in the world on a variety of topics. My knowledge base in business increased, and my contacts and relationships grew. By taking action, I was rewarded with perhaps the best resource I have ever had at my disposal. Simply giving a little bit of my time allowed me to access an organization much more valuable than any paycheck! If you are sitting back and waiting for something to fall into your lap, it's a foolish strategy. You have to take action in the direction you want to go before you will taste any success.

They say that "a body in motion stays in motion," and it is a truism for a reason. Get moving, and you may be surprised where your momentum takes you.

Take action . . .

"JUST PUT YOUR PIMP FOOT FORWARD AND LET THE OTHER ONE FOLLOW."

—SNOOP DOGG, RAPPER AND ACTOR

LIFE LESSON #4:
BE COMMITTED!

WATCH THIS CLIP TO HEAR WHAT I HAVE TO SAY ABOUT BEING COMMITTED!

love this famous Will Smith quote from an interview with Tavis Smiley:

"The only thing that I see that is distinctly different about me is I'm not afraid to die on a treadmill. I will not be out-worked, period. You might have more talent than me, you might be smarter than me, you might be sexier than me . . . But if we get on the treadmill together, there's two things: you're getting off first, or I'm going to die. It's really that simple.

You're not going to out-work me. It's such a simple, basic concept. The guy who is willing to hustle the most is going to be the guy that just gets that loose ball . . . The majority of people who aren't getting the places they want or aren't achieving the things they want to in this business is strictly based on hustle. It's strictly based on being out-worked; it's strictly based on missing crucial opportunities. I say all the time, 'If you stay ready, you ain't gotta get ready.'"

I love this quote, and I don't know if anything summarizes my approach to life as well as the Fresh Prince himself put it. If you want anything in life, you have to be willing to work your butt off to get it. If you approach your life with this kind of passion, there is nothing that can stop you from reaching your goals and living your dreams. It is a choice you have to make each and every day. Even when you are tired and want to sleep, hungry and want to eat, sick and want to go to bed . . . you have to keep pushing. Your commitment to your success has to be relentless; you have to be willing to die on the treadmill!

I've never been the most talented or gifted person at anything in my life, but my parents did instill in me the importance of hard work at an early age. Growing up, I had a long list of chores each day. Taking care of my own laundry, helping out in the kitchen, lending a hand at chopping and stacking firewood, and other daily chores were just part of life. I was taught that I had to pull my own weight and contribute by doing my fair share within the family. Developing a good work ethic has helped me out tremendously in life! Whether my work ethic was applied to school, sports, or my career, I've always made it my mission to be the hardest worker on the court. A good work ethic helps you stand out and prepares you, as well as gives you the confidence, to perform at your highest level. I attribute the majority of my "good fortune" (and what some would consider successes) to the fact that I am willing to work beyond what is expected.

As a young boy, when I watched *The Pistol*," and it had a tremendous effect on my life. The movie tells the story of Pete "The Pistol" Maravich, who was, in his day, one of the greatest basketball players to ever play the game. He grew up in the country with a dad who was a high school basketball coach who constantly encouraged him. Pete took a basketball with him everywhere.

He walked on the train tracks while he was dribbling. He even dribbled out the car windows while his dad drove him to school. One time, he spun the ball on his finger for an hour to win a bet, even though his fingers started to bleed. He would even take his basketball to bed with him and sleep with it! Pistol Pete was a shining example of being committed to being great.

> **"YOU JUST CAN'T BEAT THE PERSON WHO NEVER GIVES UP."**
>
> —BABE RUTH, BASEBALL PLAYER AND LEGEND

I was inspired by his commitment (and the fact that he was an undersized white kid from a small town, just like me) to be a great basketball player. I began to imitate his attitude toward the game, his commitment to developing amazing skills, and his belief in himself. If you ask folks in my small hometown about me today, they would tell you I took a basketball with me everywhere! I drove my parents crazy with my antics, and I broke a ton of stuff in the house with my nonstop dribbling and messing around with the basketball. But it was that commitment, and putting in the hours of practice, which allowed me to continue to play basketball long past the time and the level of ball I should have been able to play. Building on that foundation, and continuing to push myself harder at every level, has given me the ability to continue having awesome and fun "work" experiences to this very day! What I loved about "Pistol" Pete was that he always found a way to make the work fun. If you dedicate yourself to something in such a powerful way, you have to find a way to make it enjoyable! No one wants to spend all their time doing something that makes them feel miserable or that doesn't excite them. Do something you can get fired up about!

When you fully commit yourself to doing something with your whole heart, you find that the obstacles that seemed so impossible to scale are really just minor speed bumps along the road to your dreams!

Another story about commitment love involves award-winning actors Matt Damon and Ben Affleck. When they were just aspiring actors, they realized that they were virtually unemployable doing anything else. They wrote their own movie script, *Good Will Hunting*, just like Sylvester Stallone did with "Rocky", in order to create roles for themselves. Damon was so committed to making his career into a success that he dropped out of Harvard. To drop out of one of the most prestigious schools in the world to pursue an acting career shows a lot of faith in your ability and takes a lot of courage. Talk about going all in and being committed! It took revision after revision for them to finally get the script good enough to get picked up, and when a major studio did finally buy it, they laughed at the notion that Damon and Affleck would play the lead roles. In fact, they wanted Leonardo Dicaprio and Brad Pitt for the leads. At that point, Damon and Affleck borrowed another page out of Stallone's playbook: they wouldn't budge

> **"IF YOU'RE TRYING TO ACHIEVE, THERE WILL BE ROADBLOCKS. I'VE HAD THEM; EVERYBODY HAS HAD THEM. BUT OBSTACLES DON'T HAVE TO STOP YOU. IF YOU RUN INTO A WALL, DON'T TURN AROUND AND GIVE UP. FIGURE OUT HOW TO CLIMB IT, GO THROUGH IT, OR WORK AROUND IT."**
>
> —MICHAEL JORDAN, BASKETBALL PLAYER AND LEGEND

from the idea that they were going to be the leads in their own script. That decision was the big break their acting careers needed, and they were both catapulted to fame. Their commitment to themselves and their plan changed their lives forever. Commit to succeed!

Never be outworked.

'1ST
QUARTER

THE
ROOKIE DRAFT

THE EARLY YEARS— DREAM BIG!

I was born and raised on Pennock Island, a small island in southeastern Alaska. To this day it remains extremely rural: no road system, no stores, no city water or other city services. There were about thirty families living on Pennock while I was growing up, and we all lived scattered along the rocky coastline. Each family had their own little dock system poking out into the water with a couple of small boats tied up on the ends. Whenever we visited each other, it was always by boat, never by foot!

JUST A SCRAWNY
LITTLE KID WITH A
BIG DREAM!

A WINTER SHOT OF MY "WATER COMMUTING" CHILDHOOD HOME ON PENNOCK ISLAND

Our water-commuting lifestyle gave us front row seats to watch eagles, coastal birds, seals and sea lions, porpoises, and humpback and killer whales. Long before I ever got my driver's license for a car, I had to take my family's small boat every day just to get to school in Ketchikan, Alaska.

Ketchikan was the "big town" (population 14,000) located about a mile and a half across the waterway, Tongass Narrows, from my home on Pennock. I know this may seem out of the ordinary to most of you, but for me growing up, it was completely normal because it was all I knew.

I grew up with a very supportive and loving family. My parents were very encouraging, and I had an older brother and sister who both loved me and were great role models for me as well. When I was a toddler learning to walk, my older brother would roll a basketball at me and knock me over like a bowling pin. He said it would "toughen me up," and he was right. Growing up, he would never let me just win at anything. I had to earn a win honestly, even though he was nine years older than me. I loved the challenge. My desire to whip my older brother is what gave me my competitive fire and love for sports at a young age. I guess I was an underdog from day one.

ME AND MY "BULLY," MY OLDER BROTHER, LUKE

I admired my brother, and I'd often go watch him play his high school basketball games in a packed house. I loved the energy that I felt at those games, especially the way the crowd would yell and scream when someone scored. This turned me on to sports and lit my competitive fire. Growing up, I was always 110 percent into whatever sport was in season at the time. I always had a ball in my hand, whether it was a basketball, a baseball, or a soccer ball. I can't even begin to count how many free throws I shot, baseballs I hit, and hours I spent juggling a soccer ball.

Very early on, I learned the importance of hard work and repetition to develop muscle memory. I wanted to be the best, and I knew that would require hard work and total dedication.

I excelled in all the sports I played. My coordination and quickness were highly developed for my age—probably a result of all the time I spent playing with my older brother—and I had a blast playing on state champion teams in Little League baseball. I was a left-handed second baseman, if you can believe that. Luckily, I was fast enough that I could still turn a double play. Though I was never a power hitter, I could make contact with the best of them, and I was a terror on the base paths! My footwork was always good, and that helped me be a tough soccer player, too. Out of all the sports I played, I was probably naturally the best at soccer. I could get around people without much effort, and I loved to pass! There is something about setting someone up to score that I always found even more rewarding than scoring myself. I loved to anticipate where the defenders and my teammate would be, then put the ball in the perfect place for him or her to kick it in.

But for me, every other sport was just conditioning for my true love: basketball.

I wanted to be known and remembered as a basketball player. It was probably because I wanted to be just like my brother Luke, who also had a passion for the game. He told me soccer was for girls (not true, but he was my big brother), and being left handed, I knew I could only play the infield for so long before I would be forced to switch to a new position. But regardless of the pros and cons of playing other sports, I always knew I loved basketball best. Plus, basketball was a great choice because it was so cold and dark in the winter in Alaska. That made it tough

AGE 9, LOVING THE COMPETITION ON MY ALL-STAR TEAM WITH BUDDY JOHN PENNINGTON

to get into outdoor sports, and being in the warm gym was a great way to pass time and have fun when it was too cold to be outside. So basketball it was, and I was determined that nothing was going to stop me from going as far as I possibly could.

Given that I was an undersized white guy that couldn't jump to save his life, basketball was the *last* sport I should have picked! When I was ten years old, I made it my goal to play college basketball. Coming from a little island in Alaska and lacking size, I knew this was a very lofty goal. But at that age, I didn't yet know what I couldn't do, so I started doing things to help me become the best basketball player I could be.

In the fourth grade, I wrote out a workout routine that looked something like this:

- 100 calf raises
- 100 right-handed shots
- 100 left-handed shots
- no sugar
- no pop
- no ice cream
- no coffee (I heard it stunts your growth, and I couldn't afford to lose any inches!)

It didn't matter what the circumstance were, I never missed a day in my routine. I realize now that it was borderline crazy to put those kind of expectations on myself at that age, but that was something I knew I needed to do if I wanted to reach my dreams. I wanted to work harder and be better! I didn't care about fitting in; I knew where I wanted to take my life, and if other people didn't like that about me, it was none of my business. Like the famous saying goes:

"I DON'T KNOW THE KEYS TO SUCCESS, BUT I KNOW THE KEY TO FAILURE IS TO TRY TO PLEASE EVERYBODY."

When you know where you want to go, don't let anything or anyone—even yourself—stop you from getting there. When I got to sixth grade my "daily basketball to-do list" started to include things like pushups, crunches, and jump rope. As I grew, so did my list of daily expectations for myself. If I felt something would give me an edge over the competition, then I would do it. It wasn't easy, but I was determined, so I pushed myself to do hard things, and I saw results. Most people walk down the center of the sidewalk; I would (and still do) walk on the uneven edge and cracks in the street to strengthen my ankles. You can think of that literally and metaphorically. I believe success in life is all about creating good habits, and if we get in the habit of doing things to improve ourselves, we'll improve. That's the simple truth. When we push ourselves out of our comfort zone, especially when it's difficult, we will find ourselves stretching and growing —physically and mentally.

In Alaska, we have a shooting competition every year called the Elks Hoop Shoot. You take 25 free-throw shots, and they total the amount of baskets you make and compare it to all the other kids in the state. In sixth grade, I went to try my luck.

I was so small that I couldn't just stand there at the free-throw line and shoot it like all the other kids; I actually had to jump. All my practice paid off, though, because I still made 23 out of 25, which was the highest score in the state of Alaska that year, so I got to travel to Portland, Oregon, and compete in the regional contest. I had one month to train, and in that time, I prepared by shooting over 10,000 free throws with my dad (the world's best rebounder). I remember making 77 baskets in a row one time, and then going on to make 99 out of 100. Not too bad for a twelve-year–old kid!

At the regional competition, all of the other competitors were much bigger than me. I noticed none of them had to jump like I did. I remember stepping

AGE 13, 2ND PLACE IN THE ELKS NW
REGIONAL HOOP SHOOT

up to the line and draining my first 8 in a row. I hit my 9th shot, too, but the referee said, "No count. He stepped on the line." I went on to hit 22 out of 25, but the one shot that didn't count cost me the competition. A kid named Lucas Snodgrass (how do you ever forget a guy with a name like that?!) made 23 . . . and he went on to the national competition. Bummer. The real kicker was that the winner at nationals got their name put in the basketball Hall of Fame! I missed my

big opportunity to get my name in there, but who knows, maybe another opportunity will come along some day. I went on to win the Elks Hoop Shoot competition for Alaska one more time, but once again I lost at the regional shoot. I felt better about it, though, because fellow Alaskan Trejan Langdon, who went on to play in the NBA, lost three times at regionals. In the end, I just counted my blessings because all four competitions were amazing experiences!

When I got to junior high, the other kids kept growing, but I didn't. My skills on the court always seemed to make up for it, though. What I lacked in height I made up for in hustle, toughness, heart, and hard work. By this age, I was staying after practice doing sprints by myself, going through full-speed ball handing drills, and putting up shots. Not too many kids want to push themselves until it hurts doing sprints—or anything else. I knew no one was doing it on my team, but I always thought there might be someone somewhere working harder and getting the edge on me. (I learned that from the "Pistol" Pete movie.) I was dedicated, and I wasn't going to let someone work harder than me! If you saw me at this age, you would probably think it was almost comical. You would see this scrawny little guy out there on the court, smaller than everybody else, hitting shot after shot, making behind-the-back passes, and dribbling in all kinds of crazy ways.

You actually can see it!

> **EVERY TIME YOU MAKE A CHOICE, YOU'RE DECIDING WHO YOU'RE GOING TO BE. GOOD CHOICE OR BAD, RIGHT CHOICE OR WRONG, SMALL CHOICE OR BIG. EVERY CHOICE ULTIMATELY DEFINES YOU."**
>
> —DONEE BILDERBACK-LEBEAU, MY MOM

CLICK THE FOLLOWING LINK TO SEE ME PLAYING "AMONG THE GIANTS" IN JUNIOR HIGH.

I won the MVP of the tournament, and my team were crowned the champions!

"ALWAYS TURN A NEGATIVE SITUATION INTO A POSITIVE SITUATION."

—MICHAEL JORDAN, BASKETBALL PLAYER AND LEGEND

LIFE LESSON #5: ATTITUDE IS EVERYTHING

HERE'S A QUICK CLIP OF ME TALKING ABOUT WHY YOUR ATTITUDE IS SO IMPORTANT, CHECK IT OUT!

ne of the biggest lessons my father passed down to me early on was that "attitude is everything." To this day, these are some of the most powerful words of wisdom I have ever received. Every day of our lives we are faced with actions, and we get to choose our reaction. We can decide how to act in *any* situation. How cool is that? Even when the chips are down and the ball isn't bouncing our way, we can choose to be happy. No one can steal that from us. The choice to live an amazingly fulfilling life is up to one person and one person only—you. One of the most important decisions you can ever make is simply this: take ownership of your life, and be the master of your own attitude. It's a choice, and ball is in your court. Choose wisely.

Sports beautifully illustrate the importance of attitude. If you've spent any time at all in the sports world, you know that you fail all the time in sports—usually more than you succeed. The best baseball players in the world are able to get a hit only 30 percent of the time. This means that a major league baseball player, who gets paid millions of dollars and is the best at his profession, fails at his job at least seven out of ten times. The best basketball players in the world are considered great if they make even half of the shots they attempt!

I've played a ton of sports in my life, and even though I was a good athlete, I spent much more time losing than I ever did winning. But losing in sports teaches us how to win in life. If you fail to see the bigger life lessons that sports are meant to teach us, and what they reveal about our character, then you've missed the boat completely. So you lost the big game, you missed the big shot, dropped the critical pass, fumbled the routine grounder, or (fill in the blank). What are you going to do now? Are you going to scream at the referee? Yell at your teammates and blame them? Say it's your coach's fault? Never play the sport again? Walk away with your tail between your legs? Tell people you don't care in order to save face? Punch the wall? Throw your glove? Give up and quit? This may sound funny, but I've seen every single one of these things happen more times than I can count. If you are a close observer like I am, then I'm sure you have seen it, too.

Growing up, I was taught to look at things differently. I was less concerned with the mistake that was made and more interested in how the situation was handled. What did the tough moment reveal about the person's character? Is this person the master of his or her attitude? This really tells me who is going to be a winner in the end. True winners run off the field after striking out and high-fives their teammates, even if they don't feel like it. They miss the line drive and immediately turn and sprint after the ball to the fence and get it into the infield as quickly they can. They drop the pass and run back to the line and get ready for the next snap, and the next day they stay after practice and do more drills so they don't make the same mistake. They miss a big shot and keep their head up because they know that failure is a part of sports. More importantly, they know that failure is a part of life. Losing a game doesn't make you a loser. The difference between a winner and loser is all in the attitude. Winners choose to embrace their mistakes and become better because of them. Losers don't.

By the time I was in Little League baseball, my parents had instilled in me the importance of hustle and having a good attitude. I can honestly say I was a great Little Leaguer. Anyone who knew me during this time period would agree. I encouraged every one of my teammate's non-stop, I sprinted to and from the dugout between innings and after strikeouts, and I never gave up on a play. I was the kid that every coach wanted his players to be like. I wasn't born with these qualities, but I was taught they were a choice.

I remember one game in particular that I had to force myself to make the right choice, and it wasn't easy. We were playing my good friend Tyler's team. It was down to the last couple of innings, and we were down by 2 runs. I came up to the plate with 2 outs and the bases loaded. This was our big chance to make our comeback and win the game. Tyler was pitching, and there's something you should know about Tyler: he was a man-child. We were twelve years old,

ME AND GOOD FRIEND TYLER RICHARDSON AT THE LITTLE LEAGUE STATE CHAMPIONSHIP GAME IN SAN BERNARDINO. I'M STANDING ON HIS CLEATS TO LOOK A FEW INCHES TALLER!

and Tyler was 6'3" and 185 pounds, and he threw the equivalent of 90 MPH in Little League. I was about 4'10" and maybe 100 pounds soaking wet . . . maybe!

I was a good contact hitter and extremely competitive, and I expected myself to get the big hit and win the game for us. As you probably guessed, I didn't get the big hit. In fact, I struck out swinging. That was over a decade ago, and I can still feel the rage I felt when I swung and missed that last pitch, basically losing the game for my team. I wanted to yell, throw my bat, kick the fence so badly, but I knew that wasn't the right response. I ran off the field and hit my coaches' and teammates' hands, grabbed my glove, sprinted out to second base, and got ready to play.

Was that easy to do? No! Was that what I wanted to do? No way! Was I throwing several choice words around in my head? Yes! But at age twelve, I knew how winner's acted, and winners didn't dwell on their mistakes; they learned from them and got ready for the next play. To me, this story illustrates why I was a winner better than any state championship, award, or scholarship ever could. Make yourself do the right thing, even when you don't want to (especially when it's the last thing you want to do), and you, too, will be a winner—no matter what life's scoreboard reads. You are going to continually strike out in life, but you have the ability to choose your response. Choose to be a winner, and find the positive in the situation.

Looking incompetent is what most athletes fear, and that's hilarious to me. I see it all the time. I still play basketball almost every day, and I play with some unbelievably talented players who are the masters of their attitudes, and most of them are also very successful in their lives, I might add. I also come across many people who don't have this principle figured out. Every time they miss a shot, you would think it was the first time they have ever missed in their life. They have to cuss and yell and act all surprised to let everyone know they are really good and it is purely a fluke that they aren't playing well. This is the same reason some people blame the refs, coaches, their teammates, faulty equipment, etc. They only care about saving face. A winner knows this is just wasted energy.

As a player, I love it when my opponent gets frustrated and argues about a call or yells at a teammate. Why? Because that is when I know I have him beat. I know that when it comes time to make the critical play, I will be more focused to do what it takes, while my opponent will be too distracted to succeed. Discipline yourself not to waste time or energy on bad plays. Instead, embrace them by immediately forgetting about a terrible call the ref made, forgetting the bad pass your teammate threw over your head and into the bleachers, and hustling back on defense after you turn the ball over. I find that if I haven't been wasting my energy to "save face" the whole game, I have that extra little bit of fire and focus (not to mention energy) that allows me to make the big play at the end of the game.

Look to develop a strong, focused, and good attitude. If you take your mistakes in stride and stop blaming others, you can focus on becoming better and making life's next "play" to the best of your ability. In my life, I've benefitted tremendously from having a good attitude. For one, I am (for the most part) obnoxiously happy, which is a great way to live life! Even when the chips are down, you can look around and find others who have it a lot worse and would love to be in your shoes. This has taught me to be grateful for what I have. Having a good attitude also attracts people to you! Nobody wants to be around a "Negative Nancy" who's always taking a trip to "negative town." People want to be around others that are upbeat; it makes them feel good! I choose to have a good attitude. I've had to work at it, so now it's a habit. You can do the same thing! Choose to find the positive and be happy; it's the best way to live!

HERE IS AN AMAZING TALK BY TONY ROBBINS, A WELL-KNOWN LIFE COACH AND MOTIVATIONAL SPEAKER, ON THE POWER OF A POSITIVE ATTITUDE.

LIFE LESSON #6: VISUALIZE IT!

HERE IS A VIDEO I SHOT TALKING ABOUT VISUALIZATION!

 ne principle I learned about at an early age was the power of visualization. I started putting this to practice during my Little League years. Back in the summer in Alaska, there was nothing I loved more than baseball. I used to spend hours upon hours shagging fly balls and grounders with my dad on the dirt field (more like a fine gravel; we couldn't get grass to grow up in Alaska). We'd play pepper, working on hitting and my favorite, the "drag-bunt." I can't even begin to calculate how much time I spent throwing a tennis ball off the side of the house and scooping it up over and over again. I was serious about the game and wanted to be the best I possibly could. Through my research, I learned about visualization and decided I wanted to try it. During the days leading up to my games, I would lay down on the bed, close my eyes, and visualize myself against the team we were up against. I would see the colors of their jerseys, the players on the field, the people in the stands. Then I would imagine myself in all the situations I would find myself: at the plate, fielding grounders at second base, and running the base paths. I would see myself doing all the things I would do in the upcoming game with positive outcomes. I always got the hit, always beat out the bunt, and always dove and made the play to get the runner out. Just as important, I imagined the way it would feel when I got the game-winning hit and when I made the diving play, and I physically felt the emotions.

In my Little League career, I only made four errors, and I attribute that to putting the power of visualization to practice. I was just a kid, but visualization made all the difference. Studies today show that your body cannot tell the different if the emotional sensation you are feeling is self-induced or caused by a real-life situation. By making your body feel that it has succeeded before you even begin, you give yourself confidence and peace. This helps you to be able to focus on your tasks without being sidetracked by these emotions that can prevent you from being successful. By doing this, I was able to be much more at ease and clear-minded when I played, which in turn made me play better and

> **"WHERE THERE IS NO VISION, THE PEOPLE PERISH."**
>
> —PROVERBS 29:18

made games more fun. Doing your best and being successful sure is a lot more fun than the alternative, isn't it? I still use visualization in my life to this day to build my confidence and plan for success.

You can apply this technique to any aspect of your life. It may be an upcoming test or a relationship with a parent or partner. It could be your career or a big music performance you committed to doing at your local church. Whatever it is, visualizing yourself performing to the best of your ability will help you in your endeavors.

This leads me to a similar topic: self-fulfilling prophecies. As the saying goes, "As a man thinks, he is." We are what we think. The power of the human mind, conscious and subconscious, is astounding. One of the biggest thing that keeps people from being successful is that they fail to believe in themselves.

Research has shown that we respond to what our brain *assumes* is going to happen next based on previous experience. There have been countless studies done that prove this theory. Doctors in different parts of the United States have done trials with patients who have worn-out joints that need to be replaced. Some of the people were put under for surgery but no procedure was done to actually improve the joints health. The doctors just made an incision to leave a scar. The crazy thing was that the people who weren't actually treated reported the same results and benefits as the people who actually received the operation. The same experiment has been performed using placebo (or fake) pills: people claim to be cured and to have experienced drastic changes in their health, despite never really taking medicine. Because the brain expected these improvements to take place, they did! It's pretty amazing how powerful our mind can be! Think if you could harness this power to reach your goals and dreams? Well, the good news is, you can!

Our brains are conditioned to expect what is going to happen next, and this doesn't matter if it actually happens that way or not. It's all based off of past experiences, and this is why, more often than not, we achieve pretty close to what we thought we would. This gives us so much power if we choose to think positively and expect GREAT results from ourselves. The beauty of it is the

> "I ALWAYS WANTED TO BE SOMEBODY, BUT NOW I REALIZE I SHOULD HAVE BEEN MORE SPECIFIC."
>
> —LILY TOMLIN, AMERICAN ACTRESS AND COMEDIAN

mind starts to do the work for you and believes and expects those bigger and better results you actively chose. Dream big and believe it, and your brain will actually help you achieve it!

Learn to Visualize.

2ND QUARTER

HARD WORK

JR./SR. HIGH SCHOOL YEARS

n some ways, junior high was a dream come true for me. *Finally*, all the elementary schools in my small town funneled into one middle school, and the chance to try out for the Knights, the junior high basketball team, was finally here. I was finally able to be on a team with all the terrific athletes I had played against in K–6 grades, and it was amazing! We had a very strong team that beat nearly every school we were pitted against in those years, and that same group of athletes stayed strong right up through high school . . . going on to win two 4A regional victories that took us to the state tournament in my junior and senior years of high school.

I was a very innocent kid, especially in junior high. I wasn't too interested in girls, yet; I was too busy with sports and trying to get A's in all my classes. As you well know, kids at this age can be a real handful. I used to come home from school and cry because "the kids at school were cussing." One class that was a real problem was my health class. Kids used to say the most graphic things, and for some reason the teacher loved it. That was not my style, and it made me very uncomfortable. I was lucky to have a healthy niche in sports during those awkward adjustment years, and I spent even more time in the gym perfecting my craft with my like-minded athlete friends.

My freshman year of high school we moved to Alpine, California for two years. My grandparents were getting older and needed more of our attention, so my mom got a teaching job as a seventh grade geography teacher, my dad commuted back and forth to Alaska for his job, and I enrolled in high school. Now, instead of hopping in my boat and running across the Tongass Narrows to get to school, I had to drive 30 minutes on different freeways. It was a far cry from the two-lane roads and four stoplights in the whole town type of driving I was used to, but all in all, it was a fairly smooth transition. I was a likable, upbeat kid, and I found that I rather liked all the pretty California girls!

I got right to work in the gym, spending hour after hour practicing before school, during lunch, and after school. The campus shared the gym with a college team, so I was exposed to really good players, which was great for me! I got to play with them sometimes and see the way they practiced. There were some talented kids in the high school, and it looked like it was going to be a good varsity team.

Even though I was a 5'4", 125-pound freshman going up against seniors who were Division 1 bound, I expected to be on the varsity team. I knew the coach a little bit because he always saw me in the gym. The day before tryouts, I found him and asked him which tryout I should attend. I didn't want to seem cocky showing up for the varsity tryout as a new kid, even though I knew I was good enough to make the team. To my delight, Coach Hoff said I should come to the varsity tryout. I was pumped!

I went on to play on the JV team, practice with the varsity, and sit on the bench for the varsity games. Our team was really good, so we usually led the other team by a lot. So come the 4th quarter, I usually got to play. Coach Hoff was a great coach, and he would usually run a play so I would come off a double screen for an open 3-pointer. I probably shot about 80 percent on those attempts, and I think the roof about flew off with the reaction I got from the home crowd. Something about a tiny white kid looking out of place on the court really got people excited. It became kind of routine: the coach would put me in toward the end of the game, I'd hit that three-pointer, and people would go nuts. I had regular fans in the stands who would get so excited for me and yell all kinds of crazy things. It was definitely a blast for me!

I remember one game I got in with about three minutes left, and I hit one shot, then another, then another! After each bucket, the announcer would shout out, "That's Jesse LeBeau, with X amount of points, a new career high!" I got to the free throw line and hit the first and the announcer went into his commentary and one of the other team's players yelled at his team angrily, "Don't foul him again! We don't want any more career highs!" I think I ended up with 14 points that game, and I was psyched!

Basketball has allowed me to meet some really cool people over the years and develop amazing friendships. That freshman year in California, I became best friends with our star player, Moulaye Niang. Moulaye was straight out of Senegal, Africa. He was 6'11" and darker than night. As a senior, he had already signed with Kansas University and had quite a presence on the court. We became close, and we were quite a pair; people would stare at us and ask for pictures

MY BEST FRIEND AND VARSITY TEAMMATE IN HIGH SCHOOL, MOULAYE NIANG. "AMONG THE GIANTS," RIGHT?

when we were out in public.

After a good freshman year, several of the top players graduated and a few transferred. Coach Hoff switched schools as well, so it was a new coach and a crop of younger players. The varsity team was pretty weak that year, but I still had a lot of fun. The new coach, Coach Tobin, was hilarious on and off the court. I was playing 32 minutes a game and scoring a lot of points, but we were losing most of our games because the bench didn't really go too deep. Coach Tobin showed a lot of confidence in my point guard ability that year, and that really deepened my confidence in myself and my ability to leading a team from that position. I remember when I had to leave for a week during the season to attend my brother Luke's wedding in Hawaii, Coach Tobin teased me that he wouldn't let me go because "you're the franchise!" I loved my brother, but I hated leaving the team for that week. Honestly, though, I think it was harder on coach than on me!

I ended up leading San Diego County in three-pointers that year, and this was the first year I started to notice what I like to call 'The Professor' effect. A lot of the school's we played against were very urban (inner city) and the fans and players seemed to have very strong opinions about me just from looking at me. Once they saw that I was a starter, it seemed like they got angry and had a lot to say about the "little white boy."

I was confident in my hours of self-appointed practices and wasn't the type to back down from the challenge. I knew I didn't pass the "look test," but the great thing about that was it made me work even harder every day to prove myself. Most of the time I was able to prove myself to the fans that wanted to heckle me so badly. The best part was when those same doubters became my biggest fans by the end of the game, and they would be cheering for me! My flashy style was so unexpected to the spectators that whatever I did, I got twice the reaction someone who looked more like a basketball player would get. I call it "The Professor" effect because it's the same thing that I saw Grayson

"The Professor" Boucher experience on the And1 tour. No one expects the little white guy to be able to show up the stronger, taller, more athletic-looking athletes. But this has become my identity in so many ways.

Having to outplay bigger and stronger athletes and struggling to break through the stereotype of "who should play the game" has sculpted me into the person I am. Even to this day, I battle against the same thing almost every time I step into a gym. People still overlook me, don't take me seriously, and (at first) don't want to treat me with respect because of the way I look. When I was younger, and more hot-headed, it used to make me mad. As I matured and gained more confidence in my game and in myself, it became comical. I knew exactly what was going to happen:

I'd be in a random gym, and the guys wouldn't want to pick me to be on their team. I'd wait around, and eventually get on the court. Then I'd do my thing, and I'd hear "ooohs" and "ahhhs." Then the same people who were disrespecting me would want me to be on their team, want to know where I played, and want me to come back and play with them again. They'd end up nicknaming me "The Professor" or "White Chocolate."

I took away a valuable lesson from this. I learned that, at the end of the day, it doesn't matter if you are white, black, brown, or purple as long as you can work hard and get results. Most people in life only care about what you can do for them. It's tough, but that's the way the world works. Everyone has a talent or skill that sets them apart from other people. What is yours? Are you good at solving problems? Perhaps you are gifted at managing other people. Maybe your strength is your ability to communicate or maybe you are a first-rate salesmen. I've found the best way you can become a standout at anything is to work your butt off and believe in yourself. If you stay hungry and continue to better yourself every day, you will separate yourself from your competition and gain the edge that can make all the difference in your career and in fulfilling your dreams.

After my sophomore year of high school, my family moved back to Alaska. I wanted to finish my last two years with my friends, and I felt we would have a pretty good team. With only two years left, I decided to bump my work ethic up to an entirely new level! I woke up at 5:30 in the morning and took my boat across the Narrows in the dark, hopped in my car, and drove to school. My mom was a teacher, so I became friends with the janitor and convinced him to open the school gym for me. I practiced every facet of my game: shots, 2-ball dribbling, defensive slides, all of it. The game of basketball came very naturally to me, and my hours spent in the gym before and after school quickly separated my skill level from many of the kids my age, even though most of them were much bigger than me. Along with all my practicing at the gym, I kept up the routine I mentioned before of doing 100 calf raises, pushups, and crunches and doing 100 left- and right-handed shots before I went to bed. It didn't

"DO THE WORK OR GET A SMALLER DREAM."

—DONEE LEBEAU, MY MOM

matter if I was tired or sick, I never missed a day of personal practice. I eliminated sugar from my diet and dribbled a rubber ball around the house non-stop. This wasn't anything that my parents forced me to do; it was all something I wanted to do on my own. I couldn't say exactly how many hours I spent in the gym practicing on my own before school and late after everyone had left, but it's safe to say I basically lived at the gym. I loved it, though! Working hard, sweating, and improving my abilities and game were all things I actually enjoyed doing. I did all that extra work because I realized, early on, those were the things that the best players did. I wasn't going to be satisfied with anything less than being the best. I worked hard, day in and day out, and I was ready when the season came.

PEOPLE THOUGHT MY ROUTINE WAS AMUSING, ENOUGH SO THAT OUR RIVAL CITY, JUNEAU, WROTE A FUNNY ARTICLE ABOUT IT IN THEIR LOCAL PAPER.

Our team did great; we were well balanced, and we won the first Regional Championship in twenty years for our town. Our coach was a very funny guy, and I liked him quite a bit. He was what my father would call a "colorful character." He cussed like a sailor, and when it came to the XO's of basketball, he didn't know much. This worked out great for me, though, because it allowed me to have a great amount of input on what plays we would run. I got to feel games out and make the adjustments on the court, and he trusted me enough to let me do so . . . and call plays accordingly.

Coach liked to run the heck out of us, so he got us in great shape! He was a great motivator; he could yell and scream and push guys buttons to get them to play hard. Most of the time, the things he yelled had nothing to do with basketball . . . and that was pretty funny to me. Before games, he wouldn't say one thing about what offense or defense we were in, or anything about a scouting report for the other team. Instead, he would yell things like, and I quote, "You gotta play like crazed dogs tonight!" and

NEWSPAPER SHOT OF A 3A-4A CROSSOVER GAME MY SENIOR YEAR AT REGIONALS WITH ONE OF THE MANY "GIANTS," 6'9" DAMIEN BELL-HOLTER (WHO IS NOW PLAYING WITH THE BOSTON CELTICS).

"We are going to rip their heads off and boil them!" He was a little bit crazy, but this strategy did get us fired up, and we played well . . . so maybe he was a genius coach after all.

Senior year came around and went pretty much the same as the previous year had gone. I worked my butt off every day before school, was still doing my workout routine from fourth grade, and was running ramps late into the night and doing defensive slides in the snow. I was hungry! I had several memorable moments; one that really stands out is our senior night, a game to honor the graduating seniors.

I had 30 points and a bunch of ridiculous behind-the-back, no-look passes. It was the game of my life; I couldn't miss from 30+ feet. On one shot, I spun at the free throw line and mid-stride, with my back to the basket, threw the ball blind over my shoulder at the basket. *Swish!* The crowd went nuts on that one! In many ways, it was a lucky shot, but one parent of a kid I worked out with thought otherwise. He told me, "Jesse, that wasn't luck; that was the reward for all your hard work." I learned another lesson right then: hard work really does pay off in the end.

We went on to win Regionals again, but we lost for the second straight year at state to Mario Chalmers's team. Now he plays in the NBA for the Miami Heat. It was fun to match up with Mario because there was a lot of hype about him being the number one point guard in the nation. He had 13 points on us, but I scored 13 points against him. I don't think he played his hardest, though; it always seemed like he would just coast through the games in high school. But I still like to tell people that we both had 13 points, so that could be me out there playing with LeBron right now if I wanted to!

LIFE LESSON #7: THERE'S NO SUBSTITUTE FOR HARD WORK!

CHECK ME OUT IN THIS VIDEO DISCUSSING HOW YOUR WORK ETHIC WILL MAKE OR BREAK YOU!

 e live in a funny time. It seems like a vast majority of the population has a huge sense of entitlement. This "me first" attitude drives me nuts.

"My parents owe me a college education."

"My government needs to provide me with free health care."

"I should start on my school's sport team because I'm a junior."

"My dream job should just fall into my lap right out of college."

It's really sad that our culture has produced such lazy and unrealistic expectations. Our grandparents used to work harder than many of us can even imagine their entire lives, sometimes barely scraping by to provide for their families. Today, many kids can't get their hands dirty and would rather play video games. We reward degenerates in our society and pay them ungodly amounts of money to be on shows like *Jersey Shore*. They become famous because the media glamorizes a lifestyle of promiscuity, laziness, and filth. We all want a big payoff in our lives, but so many of us don't want to pay the price personally! Newsflash: there is no substitute for hard work. If you want something badly enough, you will have to make many sacrifices along the way in order to get it.

> ## "YOU CAN'T HIRE SOMEONE ELSE TO DO YOUR PUSHUPS FOR YOU."
>
> —JIM ROHN, ENTREPRENEUR AND MOTIVATIONAL SPEAKER

I've had some pretty exciting doors open for me in the world of entertainment: commercials, movies, jobs, and sponsorships. If you think that all of this just happened overnight because I got lucky and showed up someplace at the right time, you couldn't be more wrong. I've been preparing myself for these kind of opportunities my entire life.

Growing up on a small island, I was forced to keep myself busy with both work and entertainment. Early on, I fell in love with soccer, baseball, and basketball, and I occupied myself for countless hours playing and practicing. I looked up to my big brother, Luke, who was a local star on our high school basketball team. Watching Luke at his games made me want to be just like him, so I began to copy everything that he did!

As I mentioned before, the movie "The Pistol: The Pete Maravich Story," was a real inspiration to me when I was young. It was exciting to see how a young boy from a small town (just like me) practiced and became one of the greatest basketball players in the world. One line in that movie really hit home to me:

"WHEN YOU'RE NOT PRACTICING, THERE'S SOMEONE OUT THERE IN ANOTHER CITY, IN ANOTHER GYM, GETTING BETTER THAN YOU ARE."

Wow! What a revelation! I needed to get to a gym—ASAP! That was when I made an important goal: "I'm going to go to college and play basketball on a scholarship." I was determined not to let anyone outwork me, no matter how long and hard I had to practice . . . and I'm willing to bet that no one did.

Being the best I could possibly be almost became an obsession for me, and that determination motivated me to get up every day in high school at 5:30 a.m., take my little uncovered boat across the Tongass Narrows (usually in terrible, freezing-cold weather), and work on my skills before school. Did I always want to get up and do it? No! But I knew that in order to get a college scholarship at my size, I had to work that much harder, so I did.

> "EVERYBODY WANTS TO BE FAMOUS, BUT NOBODY WANTS TO PUT IN THE WORK!"
>
> —KEVIN HART, ACTOR AND COMEDIAN

When team practice came along, I don't think I ever lost a sprint. If the coach said to get on the line, I sprinted and was always the first one to get there. I knew I had to do things right and develop good habits. I couldn't be worried about being "cool" or what anyone else was thinking about me. I wanted to win every drill, and I would do whatever it took every day. I didn't always beat everyone, but I always had the drive and desire and determination to try. I always gave 100 percent. Each time I hustled, even in between drills, I knew I was reinforcing a great work ethic. If I wasn't willing to sprint to get water, grab a loose ball, or get to the free throw line, what would push me past being just a good athlete into being a great one?

I've observed that successful people, whether in sports, family relationships, or business, do things differently. Those subtle (or not-so-subtle) differences separate them from the pack. Whether it's training harder, dedicating more nights a week for family time, or implementing new strategies into their businesses, successful people develop great habits and practice them consistently.

> **"SMART PEOPLE LEARN FROM THEIR MISTAKES, BUT THE REAL SHARP ONES LEARN FROM THE MISTAKES OF OTHERS."**
>
> —BRANDON MULL, AUTHOR

Begin observing people you admire, and learn from them. You don't have to reinvent the wheel. Expose yourself to new ideas, values, and practices. You should never stop learning throughout the course of your life. If you get to the point where you think you know it all and no one else has anything to teach you, you need to give yourself an attitude adjustment . . . because you're wrong.

I've had some great coaches over the years, and also some that weren't so great. But even the coaches that lacked knowledge of the game gave me little golden nuggets of truth that I benefited from. In other areas besides sports, I have often found that a person who has made bad decisions in their life has deeper insight into problems and can provide a more powerful perspective to me because of their mistakes. It is true that hindsight is 20/20. Never write people off.

To this day, I try to be like a sponge and absorb all the information I can from different people I come across. If you have a goal you want to reach faster, learn shortcuts from others. Mistakes waste valuable time (even if you learn from them), but if you observe and apply what successful people are already doing, your time to a goal can be shortened. Personally, I don't like wasting my time, energy, or money. Try actively seeking out advice from others, and be a keen observer of the people who are already where you want to be! That can be hard work, too. But it's worth it.

When I was in high school, I looked for even more places to practice basketball. I was able to get a key to the gym in a local church. It was an old building with a small, dimly lit court, but it was a perfect spot for me to get my practice in. When I wasn't at my school gym in the early morning or at the local rec center, you could find me at the Lutheran gym. I spent hours and hours in that gym working on my ball handling, my jump shot, and general conditioning. While many of the other guys were discovering girls and partying, I opted out and spent my Friday and Saturday nights with my little boom box in this tiny little sanctuary, sweating and perfecting my craft. I wouldn't have had it any other way. I loved the solitude, and all the hard work paid off. I knew no one else was putting in the time I was. I also knew my size was working against me, so making extra sacrifices to up my game was just what I had to do.

I always knew there were other basketball players who were more genetically gifted, more naturally athletic, and more talented than me. Many guys ended up playing at higher levels than me in college, overseas, and eventually the NBA. But the years I spent working my tail off taught me more about myself than I could have ever imagined, and those lessons have carried over to the other parts of life and allowed me to live a life I wake up excited for every day.

One of the biggest things I've learned is that nothing comes without sacrifice and hard work. I made the choice growing up to focus, sacrifice, and develop my skills in basketball, and that has led me to where I am today. And it may just be symbolic, but I still have the key to that little Lutheran gym to this day.

LIFE LESSON #8: GET SELF-MOTIVATED!

IN THIS VIDEO I SHARE WHY YOU SHOULD BECOME SELF-MOTIVATED.

There's no substitute for hard work.

In order to get to where you want to go, you have to possess an inner self-determination. Nobody said it was going to be easy. If it was, then everybody would be doing it. Many kids have parents who are the driving force behind their pursuit of greatness. Having supportive parents is a wonderful thing, and something I was very blessed to have growing up. But some parents are doing too much. Whether it's in sports, academics, music, or anything else, when a parent is the driving force mandating practice or study time the kid can often be driven away from, rather than towards, a goal. A perfect example of this is on those reality shows where stage moms are trying to turn their little girls into pageant winners. What may have started out as a fun little pursuit between mothers and daughters becomes all about the moms living vicariously through their little girls. Pretty soon, young Susie has had enough, and Mom is now resorting to "Smile pretty and do what I say, and I'll take you to McDonald's when we finish." Yeah, there's a good strategy!

If you really want something bad enough, you have to grow a passion where you're willing to do anything to get the edge. When you feel passionate about something, you could work hard on it for hours on end, and it would only feel like it's been minutes. You have to love something enough that you would do it for free.

Growing up in Alaska and commuting by boat, I spent a lot of time going up and down ramps. The tides are huge up there, changing more than twenty-five feet. You could tie your boat up to the dock at one time of the day and walk up a virtually flat ramp. Later in the day, when you come back, you might have to deal with a ramp that is nearly vertical! I spent a lot of time running these ramps for conditioning. It was tiring, but I was committed to it. There were many nights when practice got out late, around 10 p.m. Despite being tired from the practice, I would put my headphones on and run up and down those ramps again and again and again, often in freezing temperatures. I wanted to get better, and I was willing to make the sacrifices. After running my up-and-downs on the ramps, I would do defensive slides on the dock.

There was a bar located up above this particular ramp, and the drunks found my workouts very amusing. They were never shy to give me their input, and it was usually not flattering. This taught me a great lesson: in order to succeed, you have to stop caring about what other people think of you.

I knew at a young age that I wanted to use basketball as a tool to get as far as I possibly could. By choosing not to listen to what negative people had to say, and not worrying about what they thought about my choices, I have been able to make some of my wildest dreams come true! The drunks actually helped spur on my practice. You can always find the positive in a bad situation; you just have to look for it! While others were at the bar and kids my age were choosing to party, I chose to do my own thing so I could get to where I wanted to be. Many of these same people are at the same places doing the same unproductive things to this very day. It's easier to stay in a familiar and comfortable place, but if you want to pursue a bigger purpose and chase after higher goals in your life, dare to be different and get motivated! Doing your own thing and reaching your goals is an exciting process. If you choose to be different and self-motivated, you will be able to enjoy the rewards it will bring into your life.

> **"THINGS MAY COME TO THOSE WHO WAIT . . . BUT ONLY THE THINGS LEFT BY THOSE WHO HUSTLE."**
>
> —ABRAHAM LINCOLN, 16TH US PRESIDENT

It could be in music, art, starting your own business, landscaping, or anything you want. The key is to find what you love to do and then go about discovering a way to turn that into a career. Many people hate their jobs, but they never took a chance of failing financially or were afraid of being judged by their peers. Get up, and get moving. Motivate yourself to keep pressing forward. Free yourself from caring about what others think, find your passion, and make it your reality! If you do that, you'll never have to "work" a day in your life.

Be self-motivated.

3RD QUARTER

TRIALS

BY FIRE

THE COLLEGE YEARS

HERE I AM TALKING ABOUT SOME OF THE HARD TIMES I
EXPERIENCED IN COLLEGE.

The end of my senior year in high school was a scary time for me. Even though I had several acceptance letters, and both academic and sports scholarship money, I didn't know where I was going to go to school. I wasn't even sure if basketball was still going to be a part of my life in college. Being from Alaska and being undersized, I didn't get much exposure, so that meant I didn't get a lot of looks from colleges to play ball. But I wanted to play basketball more than anything, so I narrowed it down to two schools that were interested in having me on their team: the University of Alaska in

Anchorage and Point Loma Nazarene University in San Diego. I decided on Point Loma. My two high school years playing in SD County had given me a love for the city and the weather, and I had a nice core of great friends there that I missed. I contacted the coach and let him know I was coming, and off I went!

I loved my teammates at Point Loma. They were a great group of guys and a solid team. I could tell early on, though, that I wasn't going to get a lot of playing time. I wasn't physically equipped to play at that level yet; I needed to get stronger. I talked to the coach about red shirting that year, and he said that was probably a good idea. For the rest of the season, I was a practice player and spent most of my free time in the weight room. However, despite my dedication and commitment, I could tell the coach didn't take me seriously. He didn't think I was strong enough to play at that level, so when the end of the season came, my athletic scholarship for the next year was not going to be there. The coach used a couple small incidents off the court as leverage to release me, but I knew the truth: he didn't think I was good enough.

Once again, my future was a big question mark. The assistant coach from my Point Loma team encouraged me to talk with his friend, the coach at San Diego City College. So I went to an open gym to meet the coach. The facility was amazing, but the environment was completely different than what I was used to. I was the only white guy there, and about 2/3 the size of very some talented, athletic, black players. These guys were from the hood, too. There was a lot of gang stuff going on, and on my first visit, a huge fight broke out and the cops had to come. It was intense! It seemed like my only option if I wanted to keep playing ball, so I decided to go for it. Coach Mitch liked how I played, and he could see that I "knew the game." He told me to come to the school and I could be on the team. I went back home to Alaska for the summer to work and be around family, and during that time, I never had any contact with Coach Mitch. I called him several times to see when I needed to be there, but he never returned my calls. I started to get nervous. People asked me, "Are you still playing ball?" To which I would reply, "I think so." I really didn't know if I was or not.

I arranged my class schedule and made housing arrangements, on pure faith. I prayed I wasn't wasting my time and enrolling at a school where I wasn't even going to play. I went straight to the coaches' office on the first day of school, and there was Coach Mitch. He looked at me, completely casual, as if he had been expecting me for weeks, and said, "What's up, Jess?" What a relief! Looks like I was going to actually get to have another season.

COLLEGE COACH AND LIFELONG FRIEND MITCH CHARLENES RIGHT BEFORE I SHOT THE KOBE VI SHOE COMMERCIAL. COACH CHARLENS RENEWED MY PASSION FOR BASKETBALL—I WOULDN'T BE WHERE I AM TODAY IF NOT FOR HIM.

My two years at San Diego City College playing basketball were a great experience. I was exposed to a lot of new things that broadened my horizons and toughened me up. In junior college, there tend to be many athletic guys who have the talent to play Division 1 ball, but not the grades they needed to land those schools. Some of the guys at SDCC with the most talent just didn't understand how to play the game at an organized level. We did have some tremendous athletes on our team. Many of them had pretty tough backgrounds growing up. Some were even involved in gangs and other illegal activities . . . so it could be a pretty rough atmosphere. They all seemed to have a predetermined opinion about the little white guy from Alaska on their team, and let's just say they didn't think too highly of me. Any chance they had to take a cheap shot at me or rough me up, they took it. I wasn't accepted, and I was definitely nervous about things that could happen to me on and off the court.

Luckily, I knew how to be tough. I don't believe in backing down to any-body, whether I was in Alaska playing white boys or in San Diego going up against full-grown black men. I went at my teammates hard! I wanted to earn a starting spot! But my playing hard seemed to only make my teammates angrier. I can't tell you how many times I got physically beat that season. I was grabbed by the hair and run into ballracks, and had my face smashed repeatedly into the walls on several different occasions. I was thrown to the ground, kidney punched, everything you can think of. I always got right back up, though, and went right back at them hard—in the game. I wasn't going to let anyone get the best of me. Eventually, it paid off. I earned not only my coaches' respect, but also that of my teammates. I became as close to them as any teammates I've ever had. Looking back, it's crazy to think of all the things I persevered through that season, but it taught me to believe in myself and to never give up, even when surrounded by bigger, stronger, and more talented people. I came off the bench that year and continued to work hard, hoping my time to start would come. It did! Some of the guys got into some trouble with the law, and the next thing I knew, I was starting and playing well enough to keep the spot.

In this league, I was usually the only white guy in the gym. I got used to being looked at as if I didn't belong; honestly, it wasn't a new feeling for me. I didn't pass "the look test," and people were quick to let me know that. I was immedi-ately judged based on how

CAN YOU TELL WHICH ONE I AM?

I looked (or how I didn't look), and this taught me to believe in myself all the more, and to disregard what anybody else thought about me and what I could do. Every time I stepped onto the court, I felt like I had a target on my back, and to be honest, I started to love it. Initially, it was a bit intimidating. I didn't fit the part, and fans and opposing players were not hesitant to let me know right away that I did not belong there almost every time I walked into the gym. If I hadn't spent hours practicing my craft, there is no way I would have had the confidence to believe in myself. But at the end of the day, I knew that no one in that gym had spent more time honing in their skills than I had. That's what gave me the belief in myself that allowed me to be successful.

Confidence is everything, but it can't be a false confidence; you have to be able to back it up. I've found that hard work is the best way to help your confidence grow. That applies to everything—not just basketball. Knowing without a doubt that you can perform, even in a hostile environment, will give you peace of mind. I got used to the pattern that would happen almost every game we had on the road. First, I'd get heckled by the fans, and the opposing players would talk smack to me. Then I'd do some flashy plays, and people would be surprised, and then a funny thing would happen. The people who had been harassing me at the beginning of the game would pull a 180 and become my biggest cheerleaders and advocates, even though I was on the opposite team! I guess people like to be surprised. It was an interesting transition to watch, and often the biggest smack-talker at the beginning of the game would find me afterward and say something like, "At first I didn't think you could play, but then I was like 'Who's this little white boy?' You got game!"

After this happened consistently, I started to gain even more confidence playing on the road. When people yelled negative things at me from the stands, instead of intimidating me, it did exactly the opposite! I loved the challenge. I couldn't wait to try to turn that non-believer into a fan. It was fun, and I've started to really enjoy the underdog role. It is great getting to do what I love

SAN DIEGO CITY COLLEGE TEAM PHOTO.

and show the people that underestimate me that I can hold my own. I've always been overlooked because of my size, so being able to prove myself is always a good feeling. As much as the hecklers added fuel to the fire, though, the key was to block out all of their negative comments and focus on the game. This has been a valuable lesson, and it has helped me become successful in a variety of different areas in my life. So take the opportunity to prove your haters wrong with hard work and heart, but remember: the only opinion that matters is what you think about yourself. Believe in your ability!

After junior college, it was time to go on to a four-year university, finish school, and play my last two years of basketball. Again, I faced the roadblock of being overlooked. Even though I had been an all-conference player, and won several "Player of the Week" awards, it was the "the look test" all over again. I did have a few offers, though, and I went to visit a couple small schools in the midwest. Great opportunities and great coaches, but I wanted to stay in San Diego. It felt like "home" to me, and there was a girl I wanted to be around (of course, that eventually fell through; she treated dogs like people—deal breaker!). I knew playing at a Division 1 school like University San Diego or SDSU would be a long shot, so I decided to hit up the coach from the NAIA school across town. They were looking for a point guard, and they loved me, so I was offered a full-ride scholarship. I was excited that I could continue playing college basketball and also have it finance my education. Added to that, I could stay in the city I had grown to love and stay connected with my close friends and dog-loving girlfriend.

What I did not know was that the next two years were going to be some of the most trying and frustrating years of my life. I went through some difficult times in college, and I share these stories to show that my life hasn't been all smooth sailing. I want you to see my down days, the struggles I've had to battle through, and the times I've made bad decisions out of pride and stubbornness. Maybe you can relate to some of the bumps in the road I've hit over the years. Hopefully you can learn from the good and bad ways I handled these situations. It is my hope that these stories will help get you through your tough times quicker and easier. I struggle with many of the same things you do on a regular basis. We all get down on ourselves, but the great news is that you have the choice to actually do something about it. If your life is awesome, that's great! I think it's because you've stopped making excuses and you've taken action to make your life what you want it to be. Even when you find yourself in tough situations, stop feeling sorry for yourself, get off your butt, and create an awesome life. If I can do that, so can you! The ball is in your court.

So, back to my college years. Things started off okay at the new school. To say it was a small school would be a huge understatement. It had strict rules, offered virtually no social life, and had a student body of peers pursuing interests that I really wasn't interested in. I was there to play basketball and get my degree, so that was perfectly fine with me. I had fun at the previous schools I had attended, and I still hung out with the social circle of friends I'd met there. Classes were easy for me, so I was able to focus most of my time on basketball.

The coach seemed to like me, and I made sure that I established my place as the starting point guard on the team right away.

It didn't take very long for me to realize the players on my new team weren't nearly as talented as the athletes I had been playing with at SD City College. My new teammates were a really nice group of guys, but as far as winning games was concerned, I could tell it was going to be a tough season. It also didn't take me very long to see that I had a coach who didn't know the game very well. Although he was a nice enough guy, he seemed insecure about his coaching, and that timidity carried over into the games. After playing for what I would consider some excellent coaches, it became apparent that this particular coach was still trying to learn as he went. Early on in the season, the coach decided to bring on a new assistant coach who, for the purposes of this story, we'll call "Ryan." That's when things started to get interesting.

Ryan's younger brother, (let's call him "Kevin") played on our team. As a ballplayer, Kevin was one of those guys who had a sense of entitlement and self-confidence that wasn't based in reality. He was cocky without talent and had a poor work ethic and attitude. He wouldn't have started on my high school team, but somehow he worked his way onto our team because his sister-in-law was the girls' coach. Now that his older brother, Ryan, was the new assistant coach, my gut was telling me the situation was going to turn out badly . . .

For some reason, our coach loved Kevin. He not only started every game, but Kevin led the NAIA in minutes played (not points made) at one point in the year. He was a slow, six-foot-tall player with an average set shot, and he didn't have much ability to dribble or pass. As the season progressed, it became apparent that our "star" player was consistently shooting us out of close games. He had a rotten attitude, but because coach was used to indulging him—and his brother was always there advocating for him—Kevin had no reason or motivation to straighten up, and so he didn't. He walked around with a "I'm-better-than-you" attitude, and he never felt the need to work hard when everyone else was pushing themselves at practice. If he missed shots or a bench player would be giving him the business at practice, he would say things like, "It doesn't matter; I make them in the game, and that's the only time it counts." The coach would even call a huddle after these remarks, and validate what Kevin had just said: "Kevin makes a great point. He makes the basket in the game, and that's when we need it."

I was floored by this response, and I was furious inside. Kevin was the exact opposite of everything I had ever believed made a great athlete. I grew up believing the principles of hard work, that "perfect practice makes perfect," and that heart, hard work, drive, respect, and attitude were the cornerstones of the game. I couldn't believe the things I was hearing out of this coach's mouth. It was surreal! It bothered me to be on a sinking ship when the captain of that ship didn't even know it was sinking.

As co-captain of the team, I felt I could talk with the coach about a few of the problems we were having. So, in private, I brought up some ideas on things we could do to make us a better team. I addressed our lazy practices and the lack of competitive drills. I also brought up things we could do to push each other and create a more competitive practice environment. I was fired up; I wasn't used to losing, and if I could help it, I never wanted to settle for being average at anything. Previously, at San Diego City College, I used to literally fighting with my teammates everyday because we all wanted to win so bad! It made all of us better and I loved it!

To my complete surprise and total dismay, the coach's reply to me was, "I don't want to wear you guys out for the whole season. Look at Kevin: he doesn't practice very hard, but he's a gamer, and he'll go all out in the games. The best player I've ever coached hated to practice, but he was unstoppable in games."

So there was my answer. He might as well have stabbed me in the heart with a butcher knife.

Let me get this straight: it was expected that hard work wasn't necessary for success and that things would just sort of "fall into place" come game time?

That was a first for me.

Then things really started to head downhill.

Despite all the nonsense, I didn't complain because I was still starting. I played most of the game, and was putting up decent numbers, but I was miserable. When you work hard to be a winner, it's hard to lose—especially when there are some pretty obvious contributors. Kevin continued to play forty minutes a game and take bad shots that cost us close games. It was so apparent that the team even met with the coach and tried to address the situation with him. The coach told us that we were delusional and dismissed the issue.

Kevin's brother, Ryan (the assistant coach), didn't like it when I questioned his brother, even when it was best for the team, and it became increasingly clear that he had it out for me. In one particular practice, I got matched up against Kevin. I knew what would happen: I was going to play 150 percent like I always do, and it would expose Kevin for the soft player that he was. After I stole the ball from Kevin a few times and scored on him, he got frustrated, and it started to get physical and competitive. As an athlete, I loved it; that was exactly what I was used to, and I

> "WHAT DOES NOT DESTROY ME, MAKES ME STRONGER."
>
> —FRIEDRICH NIETZSCHE, GERMAN PHILOSOPHER

believe facing tough competition is a key component to improvement. Kevin, on the other hand, didn't like it, and when a rebound came our way, he grabbed me and threw me to the ground.

I popped back up, fired up to get the ball from the obvious foul and ready to make sure my team won the drill. Ryan looked at me and said, "Where do you think you're going? Their ball; foul on you."

I had a choice to make. I could have shrugged it off, knowing that I did my best, but instead, I let my temper get the better of me, and I fired back at him,

"Are you kidding me? Because he's your brother he gets every call?"

That comment got me kicked out of practice, and I had to sit out the next game. We played the worst team in our conference, and I had to watch from the bench. I sat there and watched our team get destroyed by a terrible team that we had beaten earlier in the season. That was hard. Really hard. And that pretty much summed up the rest of the season.

This experience was unlike anything I had ever experienced. I had always been one of my coaches' favorite players because I was always early to practice, had a good attitude, encouraged my teammates, and was the last to leave. I still have great relationships with most of my past coaches, so this awful experience really left a bad taste in my mouth toward basketball. But I learned something important, something that every successful person has to face: life isn't fair. Sometimes no matter how diligently you work, no matter how hard you try, you will find yourself in frustrating situations that cause you pain and are completely out of your control. And that's just life. The key is to hang in there and keep doing your best until things turn in your favor.

I did my best to stay positive, and finally, one day, a stroke of luck came along . . . or so I thought. Our coach was fired at the end of the season, and a new coach was coming in. In the meantime, Ryan tried to assemble everyone on our team together and get them to rally for him to be the new coach. When I opted out of that, he went around and told the other players that if he became coach, his first order of business would be getting rid of me. Another classy move on his part. I wasn't surprised, though. I was confident that he wouldn't get the job, and I glad he was going to be gone so I wouldn't have to deal with anymore of their family drama. I was going into my senior season of college basketball, the culmination of my entire life's worth of dedication to my craft. I was ready for the change, and I was excited to end on a high note.

Unfortunately, this was not in God's plan for me.

Things started out well enough. As the team captain, I got to sit in on the interview process, and the new athletic director was really excited about the first candidate. We'll call him Coach Sun. Sun had a successful business background and said all the right things in the interview. He knew when to smile and laugh, and seemed like he would do a good job as the new head coach.

My life was never as miserable as it was during the five months I had to deal with this man.

He was even worse than the coach the previous year. Here were a few details I found out later on:

- Sun only had one year of varsity high school experience under his belt, and his team only won three games the entire season.
- The parents and players on his high school team gave incredibly negative feedback about his character.
- He was a self-made millionaire and didn't take a salary from our school, which is basically why he was selected for the job.

He was in no way qualified to coach at our school. He expected me to stay in San Diego over the summer to workout with the team. I explained to him that I had to go home to work, which was how I supported myself financially while at school. Strike one.

Coach Sun didn't seem to understand that some players didn't have parents who just paid for everything while their kids were in college, but he reluctantly let me go. I left for Alaska in May, but I talked with him over the summer and told him about the workouts I was doing. I was dedicated and did pushups and whatever I could on the boat, in between an already physically demanding workload as a commercial fisherman. I had to stay to finish out the fishing season, so I came back to school a few days late and was informed that we were having "tryouts." I'd never heard of anything like this, and I was pretty irritated, to say the least. We did all kinds of shooting drills and timed sprints and mile runs. I was not in my best cardio shape after being restricted to a boat for the last three months, but my determination and sheer desire pushed me to have the best score in nearly every category. I figured that no matter how much pain I felt, I could endure five minutes of running, and I did. In my mind, nothing could be worse than three months on a boat doing something I had no passion for. Commercial fishing had really helped me increase my mental toughness, and I was grateful for that.

Some of the players that came back to the school on previous scholarships were told they were not going to be on the basketball team that year. I felt bad for the players who got cut, but it was out of my control. We started practices, and despite everyone saying they didn't want Ryan to be the assistant coach, he was brought on. New Coach Sun even asked the advice of previous coaches and his mentors, and they all advised him it would be very foolish to bring this guy back on board, but he did it anyway.

Right then, I knew I was in for it. I tried to have the best attitude I could, but things began to slowly brew into the perfect storm for me.

Coach Sun had a bad combination of arrogance and lack of experience. He was going to do it his way, and wasn't going to listen to anything anybody else had to say. Even though I'd been team captain the year before, Ryan saw to it that my backup, who came off the bench, would be our team captain that year. We started the season off losing to inferior teams, and it was pretty apparent that the offense we were running wasn't going to work well with our roster. I stepped into Sun's office and tried to a positive talk with him, just sharing some of my thoughts after being in that league and playing at that level for a few years. He quickly dismissed me and got defensive; it was "his way or the highway." Basketball is a game of a thousand adjustments, much like life. The best coaches are constantly changing things up to gain the advantage over the opponent. For Coach Sun to ignore such a blatant problem as an unsuccessful offense made no sense to me. I've heard that trying to do the same thing over and over again and expecting a different result is the definition of insanity. It seemed like I was playing for the "University of One Flew over the Coocoo's Nest"!

The losses started racking up, and Sun started benching players that voiced any opinions about the offense. Everything he was decided to do seemed to be based on his ego rather than what was best for the team. He got us nice warm-up suits and iTunes cards for Christmas, trying to buy our loyalty, but I didn't want a new friend or a sponsor; I wanted a good coach. More than anything, I wanted to have a great final year of basketball. It wasn't going to happen, and I was becoming miserable on and off the court.

They say that sports don't build character, they reveal it. Through basketball, I got to learn exactly what type of person my coach was, and I got a deeper insight into my own character and priorities, as well. I realized I was fighting a losing battle. Here I was, at the peak of my career, my last year of college sports after a lifetime of dedication and hard work, and I was miserable. This wasn't how I had expected things to be, and if the coach wasn't going to make any changes, I knew I needed to—for my own happiness. I finally went to the athletic director and said I wanted out. That was one of the toughest decisions I have ever had to make. I have never been a quitter, and it was not in my DNA to throw in the towel, even when things were tough . . . but this was a good lesson for me. I discovered that there are some times in life when you have to cut your losses and move on. This wasn't so much about quitting as deciding to distance myself from such a poisonous atmosphere. I wasn't happy, even though I was technically doing what I loved most, so I decided that if the AD could guarantee that I could keep my scholarship, I was out. Thankfully it worked out, and I was able to finish the year with my tuition paid. Although I was devastated about losing the second half of my senior year of hoops, I was relieved to have my free education . . . and to be free of this ongoing circus.

I sat back and focused on school and my life after basketball. All the drama and adversity in my life that year taught me a great deal about myself, and some bigger life lessons, too. Everything happens for a reason. As bummed as I was about losing out on my last year of college ball, I knew I had to move on.

Even in the midst of such a difficult time in my life, there were a few good moments.

HERE ARE A FEW HIGHLIGHTS FROM MY COLLEGE CAREER.

When I quit the team, I was devastated, but my troubles weren't over. I was bummed that what was supposed to be my last and best year of basketball was taken away from me, that the year that I had been working toward my whole life was cut short, thanks to a couple of knuckleheads who didn't know the first thing about coaching winning basketball. I wanted revenge on them. I didn't sleep well. I started to have trouble with my vision. My inability to forgive my coaches consumed me, and I was living an extremely unhappy life.

The way I saw it, these men had robbed me of the thing I cared most about. The thing I had trained my whole life for. The thing that had motivated me every day since I was a little kid: basketball. Finally, it hit me: I'd quit the team to get away from them, but I was letting them hurt me by holding on to my bitterness. Night and day, all I could think about was how my coaches had "won" and I had "lost" by quitting. I knew I did the right thing, and I was "in the right," but that didn't make it any easier. I fought it every day, but I couldn't seem to move on. I knew what I had to do, but I didn't want to do it. I needed to forgive them, even though they didn't deserve it or ask for it. It was about doing what was best for me, and it changed everything. I decided I couldn't let them, or any of those negative experiences, have any more power over me. If I was ever going to learn to love the game of basketball again, I knew I needed to forgive them and move on.

Forgiveness can be hard, but it is such a powerful thing. Almost immediately, my vision improved. I was sleeping better, I had more clarity about my future, and most importantly, I was happy. I learned from this experience of letting go and forgiving, something new could come alive for me. It's funny, but God had bigger things planned for me that I ever could have dreamed! As for the coaches, by forgiving and not seeking revenge, I let God handle the situation, and He did. People eventually saw their true colors, and Sun and Ryan are no longer coaching.

I share these tough times with you not to vent or call out these coaches, but rather to give you the full lens of my life, good and bad, and to let you learn from my trials and mistakes. I believe those last two years of college ball happened for a reason. I learned how to be more patient and how to deal with people in positions of authority . . . even though I didn't always do it right. I learned how to forgive people who didn't deserve it and how to let go of something I thought I loved to reach for something better.

Ironically enough, it was during this hard time that I met a teammate who introduced me to a whole new chapter of my life after school . . . the commercial sports opportunities to be had in Hollywood! Although my senior year of college was a low point for me, and I lost some of my passion for the game of basketball, I was eventually able to bounce back and become a better person because of it. I firmly believe that the life lessons we learn from sports are some of the most beautiful. Sports teach us to pick ourselves up when we're down. When we fail, sports teach us to evaluate what went wrong, learn from it, and do better the next time we take a shot. When you have negative experiences in your life, don't miss the bigger picture. Very few of us go on to play ball professionally, but everyone goes on to be a professional person within their own life. Equip yourself to be best person possible, and look for the lessons you can learn in the messy business that is our lives.

LIFE LESSON #9: STAND UP FOR YOURSELF!

SOMETIMES YOU JUST HAVE TO STAND UP FOR YOURSELF. FIND OUT WHY IN THIS VIDEO!

 ometimes the right thing to do is turn the other cheek. Other times, you have to stand up for yourself. As easy-going as you might like to be, you can't allow other people to walk all over you. Believe me, if you're not careful, they will. I talked a little bit about how I stood up to my college coaches my last two years of school. I'm not saying I always did it right, but I tried to be respectful and to keep the good of the team in mind. Those were just a couple examples. I've always been "the little guy," so I've had to stand up for myself a few other times, even when doing so was less than comfortable and cost me a good amount of money.

I'm a firm believer that people can only treat us how we allow them to treat us. I don't tolerate it when people treat me disrespectfully. I try to treat everyone with whom I come in contact with a high level of respect, and I expect the same in return. I don't care if you are a junior high–aged kid or the president of the United States. Of course, there is a difference between disrespect and good-natured teasing, and believe me, I love to talk smack to my friends as much as the next guy. I am talking about the intentional attempt to demean or disregard a person's humanity by using a position of authority or social stature to do it. In a word: bullying.

As I mentioned before, I went home to commercial fish in Alaska during the summers in college. I made a solid amount of money, and in return, I had to basically give up three months of my life. Besides being a dangerous job, seining in Alaska is exhausting work, both mentally and physically. You're out in the middle of nowhere for days at a time without cell phone service, friends, family, or the ability to shower! I had no previous experience, so I had to learn a lot in a short amount of time. Growing up on the water, I was used to running a boat, so that made the transition a little easier. What I lacked in experience I tried to make up for in hustle and extra effort.

Unfortunately, fishing boat captains in Alaska are not known for their great people skills. Many are coarse, and some can have a real mean streak. Nearly all of them are self-absorbed, and because they see themselves as the top of the food chain, they feel they can pretty much treat their crew however they want to . . . and generally, no one challenges them. Almost every boat is the same. The captain holds the crew members' three-month paycheck until the end of the season, and then, when the final earnings come in, he gives each crew member the percentage of the catch he decides that they earned, within a certain range. Some guys are lucky enough to get a contract at the beginning of the season, but few captains like to sign a contract up front. That would give them less power over the crew.

My captain was a nice enough guy on the shore, but I quickly learned that on the boat he turned into another person altogether. I was the new guy on board, so he made it his personal mission to try to make my life miserable . . . and "make a man out of me." Every little mistake was blown way out of proportion, and I was called every derogatory slur in the book for no apparent reason. I assumed this was part of the initiation for a "newbie," so I just tried to roll with it.

Observing people and trying to figure out why they act the way they do is something of a hidden pastime of mine. I was in close proximity to a real character. I've never seen such a lack of leadership and communication in all my life. If I did something wrong, instead of coming up to me and saying, "Hey, you're doing that wrong. Here's how it needs to be done next time," I would get "What the heck are you doing down there? You are a worthless piece of crap and you can't do anything right!" (I may have cleaned up the language a bit.) Nothing was ever done to actually address or correct a problem. Instead, a steady stream of insults and curse words seem to be the captain's solution. I wondered why a boat captain wouldn't want to encourage his deckhands who were making him a tremendous amount of money. Why wouldn't he want to get us fired up and hustling around in a positive way? I still don't understand it.

I bit my tongue and just took it as part of my duty as the new guy on board. The other guys took it because they were afraid to get on the captain's bad side, and while this was a summer job for me, many of the crew members were trying to make a full-time living in the field of commercial fishing. So they took the abuse and stayed quiet. I don't know how they took it year after year! You could pay me a million dollars, but I'd rather go away with nothing and still have my self-respect.

Later in the season, the captain really ripped on me about counting the amount of fish incorrectly when we were delivering our catch to the cannery boat. I had gone above and beyond that day, and I knew I hadn't miscounted.

On top of that, the crew rotated jobs, but none of the other guys ever bothered to count the fish when it was their turn, so it made no sense that he was so angry at me for something he didn't even require the crew members to do.

I'd had it. I told him he was wrong. I didn't cost the boat any money, and he wasn't going to ever talk to me like that again. He didn't like it, and he got in my face, but after that, he didn't come at me anymore for the rest of the season. I felt that he took it out on me with my final paycheck, but in the end, I had established that I wouldn't allow him to treat me disrespectfully. That, to me, was worth more than any amount of money.

The next summer came around, and I decided to fish again. I figured I had just gotten on a bad boat. My older brother assured me that he had lined me up with a better boat and captain. I was willing to give it another shot because the money was good, but to my total dismay, this guy was even worse than the first captain! I've never met anyone with such a lack of social skills. On top of that, although he was making great money (six figures a year, at least), he was the cheapest person I've ever seen in my life. We weren't allowed to buy milk and various other "crew" groceries because it was too expensive, even though the money came out of the crew member's pay! I tend to be OCD with cleanliness, but this guy took it to another level. He yelled at us for sitting down the wrong way, for smelling bad after being on a boat five days hauling nets 14 hours a day, and for eating too much food. I came to the conclusion that these seine captains went back in time when we left the harbor. In their minds, they were the kings of the old ages and we were the serfs, who they could command at will.

This new captain tried to be hard on the crew right from the start, but I spoke up from day one. I had done this before, and I was not interested in living another three months in total misery. He backed off immediately, and didn't give me any more problems for quite a while. Since he couldn't ride me, it seemed like he decided to be extra hard on our eighteen–year-old "newbie" crew member, Ryan. Ryan was from Arizona and had no idea what he had gotten himself into. However, Ryan learned fast and worked hard, and he turned into a reliable deck hand. Captain Brad rode him mercilessly, and I've never seen someone treat another human being so poorly. Because this kid was out of his element, the captain thought he could just blast him for everything, day in and day out. It was disgusting. One day, the captain took a bad fall and messed up his back. It seemed like karma had struck, and sadly, none of us on the boat felt bad for him. We figured he had it coming. A new crew

> **"WE TEACH PEOPLE HOW TO TREAT US."**
>
> —DR. PHIL MCGRAW, TELEVISION PERSONALITY AND PSYCHOLOGIST

member was brought onboard to pick up the slack and perform the duties that the captain could no longer do with his injured back. That was fine with us until we discovered that the new crew member's pay was going to come out of *our* pay, not the captains! We were doing the same amount of work we had done all season. The new guy was only doing the things the captain couldn't do anymore. This captain was so cheap, he thought he could take advantage of us and not be forced to take a hit to his bottom line. I confronted him about it, and he didn't like it one bit. Not only did I tell him that it was wrong that he was trying to cheat us out of our hard-earned crew share, but I also told him that I wasn't going to allow him to treat Ryan the way he had been anymore. It didn't matter if Ryan was young, inexperienced, or anything else—he deserved the basic respect that every human being should be treated with.

Well, the captain didn't like what I had to say one bit, and that was my last day on the boat. I was paid for my work up to that point, but I missed out on the money I could have made toward the end of the season, which was about $10,000 as the salmon make their big run. This was a lot of money for me, especially as a struggling college student. At the end of the day, though, I'm glad I got canned over this issue. Like I said before, I wouldn't have stayed around this environment if he was going to pay me a million dollars. It wasn't worth being part of a crew that was treated so poorly and disrespectfully, just to get a paycheck. Looking back, I am glad I took a stand for what was right, and it encouraged me to know that I had my family's support. I knew they were proud of me for taking a stand when my dad said, "I wouldn't have respected you if you didn't stand up for what was right." When we stand up for ourselves or for someone else, we'll always be making the right choice.

Don't ever let another person talk down to you, or treat you like you are less than what you are. Every person deserves respect, and that means you, too. So treat people with respect, but don't be afraid to show others that they need to respect you.

Stand up for yourself.

LIFE LESSON #10: TAKE COMPLETE OWNERSHIP OF YOUR LIFE!

IN MY OPINION, NONE OF THE OTHER LIFE LESSONS MATTER IF YOU DON'T MASTER THIS ONE. CHECK OUT THIS VIDEO TO SEE WHY!

I n basketball, you can usually hear players say two words if you listen close-ly enough. Those two words are "My bad." Maybe a player turned the ball over, missed an easy shot, or blew a defensive assignment. Whatever the case, players are taught to take responsibility for their actions and move on to the next play. I used to take it so far as to say "My bad!" when it actually wasn't my bad, but rather one of my teammates'. A smart player does this for a number of reasons:

One, it allows your teammate save face.

Two, it can build your teammate's confidence so he won't keep making mistakes.

Three, I think it's the true sign of leadership if you're willing to take responsibility for an error that you didn't cause.

The funny part is, anyone watching who actually knows basketball will know that it really wasn't "your bad," so it isn't really that big of a deal. If taking some blame helps your teammate play better, and puts you in a better position to win the game, why not say it?!

The same is true in life. You have to run from this "woe is me" attitude. Average people have thousands of excuses for why they aren't living the life they want:

"My parents don't support me."

"I'm not smart enough."

"I don't have the proper education to get that job."

There is a saying about those who use their backgrounds as an excuse not to excel in their lives: "Sometimes you have to rise above your raising." There are so many inspirational stories of men and women who excelled in all walks of life, who "rose above their raising." Every chip was stacked against them, but they chose to make something great from their lives. While it is true that we can't change our past, nothing is stopping us from creating our future.

You probably aren't going to like this, and maybe you won't even agree with me, but I'm here to tell you this today: if you aren't happy with your life, it's your own fault. We all possess the ability to create the life we want. Stop feeling sorry for yourself, and make your life what you want it to be! Stop blaming other people! Stop making excuses! Imagine if you took that wasted time and energy and used it to change your circumstances and fix the things you don't like. What kind of life would you have then? I'd be willing to bet it would be a lot better. The highest achievers don't blame others and make excuses. They don't expect someone else to make them happy, and they don't have a sense of entitlement and expect everything to be handed to them on a silver platter. They make it happen! They start taking different action steps to get different results. This attitude is what makes all the difference between those who are great and live happy lives and those who don't.

There is only one person who is responsible for the quality of your life, and you guessed it: that person is you. Everything that is happening in your life is the result of your previous actions or lack thereof. That makes you the grand master in charge of the current state of your life. Our human nature conditions us to blame external factors that are out of our control to give us a scapegoat. But the truth of the matter is, it all comes back to how we choose to respond to each event that determines our outcome. Like I mentioned before, we can't always control the things that happen to us; the only thing we have the power to control is our attitude and how we choose to respond. The choice is yours. Take charge of your life. Think better thoughts. Visualize more positive outcomes. Take the action necessary to get what you want. This will determine everything for you and your life. Stop wasting your time being unhappy. Choose wisely, and take 100 percent ownership for your life!

In life, everybody can be a teacher for you. You never know who can teach you a valuable life lesson. Here's a few people who have incredible stories, who stepped up to the plate, stopped feeling sorry for themselves, and took complete ownership of their lives:

J. K. Rowling is best known as the genius behind Harry Potter. She has all the fame and fortune the world could offer. But before any of that happened, many people don't know that she was extremely depressed, divorced, completely broke, and trying to raise her child while also going to school. That doesn't leave a lot of time for novel writing. Rowling couldn't have been much further down on her luck, but she stood up and made the choice to take own-ership for her life. She went from barely making ends meet on welfare to being one of the richest women on the planet in only a few short years. What an amazing example for all us! Her story makes my obstacles and excuses seem pretty small, to say the least.

And we all know Jim Carey (unless you've been living under a rock) as the hilarious comedian and actor who has made us laugh for years. But before he rose to superstardom, he had insurmountable odds stacked against him. When Carey's dad was only fifty-one, he dad lost his job, and Carey, along with his whole family had to get jobs as security guards and janitors to try to stay afloat. He was going to school while working eight-hour shifts at the factory after his classes. Instead of throwing in the towel, Carey says that the desperation was the necessary ingredient for him to learn, create, and achieve. It wasn't enough, however, and on his sixteenth birthday, he dropped out of school. He was living out of a van with his family in total poverty, literally at rock bottom. Trying to help support his family, he started working the comedy clubs. His first experiences in the comedy world were awful. He was booed off stages and hissed at by angry crowds. This guy had every reason to be mad at the world, to blame others, and to give up on his dreams. But he didn't. He persevered and didn't take "no" for an answer. After moving to L.A., he drove up to a hill that overlooked the city, and visualized all the movies, awards, and money he was going to make. He started believing in it and putting those thoughts out to the universe. He then wrote himself a check for $10 million for "acting services rendered" and dated it three years ahead. Not long after that, he then found out that he was going to make $10 million doing *Dumb and Dumber*. If you can see it and believe it, you can achieve it! Take ownership of your life by visualizing where you want to be and then getting out there and making it happen!

Walt Disney wasn't always the billionaire known for movies, theme parks, and merchandise. Before any of his success, he was fired from several jobs, one from a newspaper editor position because "he lacked imagination and had no good ideas." He then tried to start several other business ventures that all failed and ended in failure and total financial loss. He didn't lose hope, heart, or belief in himself, though. He didn't blame anyone else or make excuses. He kept going and eventually built the empire we all know and love today.

Richard Branson is known today as the eccentric rebel billionaire and owner of all things Virgin (airlines, record label, phone company, etc.) who has a flare for theatrics! He is one of the wealthiest men alive today and has tons of fame and influence, not to mention his own tropical island. Growing up, he was told he wouldn't amount to much because he struggled in school and battled with dyslexia. Did he sit around and feel sorry for himself? No! Instead, he used his people skills and street smarts and proved that, with drive and focus, you can overcome the "giants" in your life and be great.

Kyle Maynard is someone who inspires the heck out of me! If you don't know who he is, you should look him up and learn more about his story. He was born with a rare disorder that stunted his growth and left him with stub arms and shortened legs. This would have left most people depressed and dependent on others to do everything for them for the rest of their lives. Kyle decided to do the opposite, and from a young age, he defied the odds and forced himself to learn how to do everything on his own. He lived by the mantra, "No excuses!" and is a true champion in life. Today, he lives to the fullest, was a great student, and became one of the top wrestlers in the state of Georgia. He holds the world record for the modified bench press at 360 pounds (way more than I can do, which isn't saying much), is an ESPY Award winner, and also won a President's Award for the Sports Humanitarian Hall of Fame. He's been interviewed by Oprah and Larry King, and is an inspiration to people all over the world. Now he uses his story to inspire others and travels around as one of the top speakers in the world. Check out his book, *No Excuses*, to learn more about his remarkable journey. It will definitely change your perspective on what you think is stopping you from getting what you want in life.

LEARN MORE ABOUT KYLE MAYNARD'S AMAZING STORY HERE.

When it comes to fame and success, there aren't too many names bigger than Oprah Winfrey. She is one of the most recognizable household names throughout the world who has impacted millions of lives with her show and work. Nothing was handed to her growing up; in fact, she had a rough go of it. She was born from a teenage single mom in a very low-income area and actually gave birth to a son when she was only fourteen years old. Her family was so poor they couldn't even afford enough clothes, and she would wear potato sack dresses. Through all of this, she still managed to work her way to the top. Had she felt sorry for herself and blamed her mom, her family, or anything else, she wouldn't have achieved the huge level of success she has today. More importantly, millions of people around the globe wouldn't have been positively affected by her. Sometimes our calling is bigger than our own fame and fortune; it's about what it will do for others. Oprah sets a wonderful example of how to take life by the horns and wrestle it into submission.

HEAR OPRAH TALK ABOUT IT IN HER OWN WORDS.

These people shared a common quality: they believed in themselves. They knew they could make it happen, and no obstacles were going to prevent them. I've had all kinds of obstacles in my way growing up, and plenty of people to remind me. I was too small to play basketball. I didn't know anything about the entertainment industry. I had no experience in writing a book. But by taking complete ownership of my life, these obstacles didn't matter. What other people say, think, and do is irrelevant. You get to decide what your life will be about. Take the first step to success by taking complete ownership for your life; blaming other's for your circumstances will get you nowhere.

Take responsibility.

HEAR WHAT JACK CANFIELD, LIFE COACH AND CO-CREATOR OF THE CHICKEN SOUP FOR THE SOUL SERIES HAS TO SAY ON THE SUBJECT IN THIS VIDEO.

OVERTIME

WHAT'S HAPPENING TODAY

MY "LIGHT BULB" MOMENT—MY LIFE'S PASSION AND PURPOSE

WATCH THIS VIDEO MESSAGE TO SEE WHY I THINK YOU CAN BE GREAT!

ne thing I am very excited about is the company I started with my good friend and mentor, Mike McClain. Mike is a very successful businessman. He has done many exciting things in his respective businesses, and I have the utmost respect for him. He even has his own private jet company, called Custom Access Jets, where people can customize and personalize their own planes. When he reached out to me, I jumped at the opportunity to partner with him and create something we both believed in: a program that uses basketball and motivational speaking to help inspire kids to follow their dreams. As I've mentioned in previous chapters, I try to practice the philosophy "surround yourself with people who are more successful than you are." This is certainly the case with my relationship with Mike. Working with him has given me the opportunity to be able to do more than I would be able to do on my own, and it gives me the chance to learn business from someone with a great track record!

Our idea was to create a team of a few select guys that had some tremendous basketball talent, had done a fair amount of work in the entertainment business (commercials, movies, television, etc.), and who could be positive role models in the community. The plan was to package this into an exciting show team that could play in games, put on shows, help raise money for causes we are passionate about, and give back to the community. What excited me most about our joint venture was that I would get to use my passion (basketball) as a means to travel and see the world, help others, inspire kids, and even make some money while I did it!

With our plan intact, I received an email asking me if I wanted to come back up to Alaska with some friends and put on a streetball game in my hometown and a few other communities. The event would raise funds for the schools' athletic programs, mostly for those teams to be able to afford to travel and compete. Unfortunately, it is extremely expensive for school sports teams in Alaska to get to the other towns for competitive games. The geography makes it very difficult as you can't just drive to your game and drive back. Athletes have to either take a day or two long ferry ride, or if the money is right and they want to be efficient, they can fly by Alaska Airlines. When I was a kid, this made for fun trips and a great incentive for kids to participate in sports.

To make the trips more affordable, coaches would fly their teams to the other team's city on a Thursday, play Friday and Saturday . . . then come back Sunday. While there, all the players would be "housed out" by the opposing team's families. You really got to know your opponents, and it was a neat way to get to know a wide variety of different people throughout the state. Although we usually didn't want to become friends with the players on the teams we were playing against because we were competitive, in the big scheme of things it was a pretty cool opportunity and unique to that area.

Well, I was excited at the opportunity to go home and give back, but also to show my new "Hollywood friends" what it was like back home. I didn't know it at the time, but this experience would changes my goals, my passions, and the overall direction of my life.

We packaged our team as The Fab4. I recruited some of my close friends who I had been in commercials and streetball games with, and we were off. These guys were excited to see Alaska and take the whole experience in. From having a snowball fight (which almost ended our team permanently after some disputes over ice balls to the face) to seeing bald eagles, the trip was a blast. We had our first show in Sitka, Alaska, in front of a pretty good crowd. I hadn't played in that gym since my junior year of high school when my team won the Southeast Alaska 4A Division Championship. Before the big streetball game, we'd gone to several of the elementary schools and had the chance to meet, play with, and speak to the students. Later that evening, with a packed gym, the show/game we put on went great! I played out of my head and had some crazy highlights, and our dunkers put on a show to remember! The crowd got really into it, too! We threw out prizes, brought kids onto the floor for dance-offs (who would have thought a little white boy all the way up in Sitka, Alaska, would win the "Gangnam Style" dance-off?), sold shirts and posters, and signed autographs after the game.

I could have never imagined the response we would get from the kids. It was the most rewarding feeling I had ever experienced! My parents flew in for the game and got to see me doing what I love to do, which made it even more special. I knew they were proud of our Fab4 team, and that they were glad they had encouraged me to pursue my dreams and goals. They had encouraged me to "take a risk," even though it was such a far, far cry from a traditional path . . . and a typical nine-to-five job.

TO SEE OUR HIGHLIGHT VIDEO FROM THE EVENT ITSELF, FOLLOW THIS LINK.

Next, we went back to my hometown of Ketchikan. People were lined up out of the building to get into the game, and we had to postpone the tip-off to accommodate the amount of people. Talk about exciting! This game was a little more competitive, which made it more fun. It was another great show, and even though I didn't have the best game, I did manage to swish a 3/4-court shot on the buzzer, which I had never done in a game before, so that was exciting! It was so meaningful to see so many people come out and support the school and also me, the "local boy." At this point, people back home had seen me on TV in commercials and streetball games and had been reaching out to me to congratulate me on the fun things I was getting to do.

It felt like this game was a big thank-you to the community for not only supporting me and my career now, but also all through my whole childhood as I pursued my dream of being a basketball player. Different folks had opened gyms up for me to practice, been my coaches, and done all sorts of things to help the youth. The local paper came and interviewed us and put an awesome article out the next day. Hal Anderson, the same photographer who used to take pictures of me in Little League, put an amazing photo of my friend Airdogg jumping over one of the cheerleaders into the spread, and the community was abuzz. So many hometowners had such a great time and thanked me during my visit. They told us that what they liked most about our show was the way we involved the students by bringing them onto the court to participate, and the way we spent time with them after the event.

The kids' response to us was amazing, and very humbling. I felt like LeBron James, signing autographs and taking pictures with so many young people! The cutest little kids had made me posters. In their own childish handwriting, they wrote out that I was their hero and they wanted to play basketball just like me someday when they grew up.

That's when it clicked. That was my light bulb moment!

I wanted to use basketball, and the blessings of being on TV and having friends of influence (with talent and platforms), to make a difference in the lives of youth!

I know I have been tremendously blessed. I had parents who loved and supported my dreams (and still do!). I had a community growing up that valued young people, and saw sports as a healthy pursuit which individuals and businesses put time and money into (and still do!). And I had the ability and drive to dribble a basketball and pursue a dream! I also know that many kids don't have those assets in their lives . . . and many never will.

My "light bulb" moment has become my purpose, my passion, and my mission in life.

On my flight back to California, the day after our Fab4 fundraiser, everything literally began to fall into place in my thinking! I knew I wanted to be an influence in the lives of kids and to inspire them to realize their dreams with hard work . . . and I was going to use basketball as the tool to tell my story.

And that's how the Fab4 Takeover was born!

With my new mission in mind, I revised the structure of our traditional streetball game and changed it to a format where we could go to schools and put on a 60-minute show. During that time, we would capture the students' attention with a crazy dunk contest, some live play against faculty and students, fun giveaways, and contests. All of this, combined with the fact the most of our players were recognizable from TV, gave us a unique approach to reach the kids and have them really listen to what we had to say. The goal was to use the "celebrity cool factor" to be able to really connect with the students. The most important part of the show was when we stopped the games and had our players speak about important topics, such as bullying, motivation, and leadership. We could use our show to really make a lasting impact, and that's what it is all about.

It has been an extremely big task to get all of this underway, one that overwhelms me at times. But I've determined that this what I'm supposed to be doing, so I am going to see it through. Often, it is scary to follow your heart and pursue your dreams. It would be much easier to go get a comfortable nine-to-five job and complete my daily mindless tasks, collect a steady paycheck, and be in the rat race. But I know I wouldn't love it. Life is short, and I want to love what I do and do something that really matters. Until you determine your purpose, you are kind of just going through the motions of life. But if you can really hone in on your purpose and find what drives you, I can say from experience you'll be ready to take bigger risks and find bigger rewards as a result.

HERE'S A SHORT CLIP FROM ONE OF OUR FAB4 TAKEOVER SHOWS.

LIFE LESSON #11: FIND YOUR PURPOSE

LEARN WHY FINDING YOUR PURPOSE IS THE KEY TO YOUR
SUCCESS IN THIS VIDEO!

After my experience in Alaska, I realized my purpose was to inspire others to examine their unique talents, reach their fullest potential, and pursue their dreams! I could do this by sharing my story as a speaker. Now that's become my internal compass, the goal that I can base decisions off of. It makes choices much easier, and I can evaluate if what I am doing is getting me closer or further away from what I want for my life. I encourage all of you to sit down and really think about what it is you want out of life.

What do you want to be remembered for? Do you want to be a great father or mother? Maybe you want to make lots of money and use it to help endangered baby birds. Remember: a purpose is different than a goal. A goal is the what; your purpose is the why. Find your purpose, and see how you can create a life based off of it. You will find that you begin to feel more fulfilled and live life with more passion than you previously knew was even possible.

By one day partnering with non-profits and major Fortune 500 companies, I hope the Fab4 will be able to impact kids for good all over the world!

SOME CUTE LITTLE FANS AT A CHARITY GAME IN WOODLAKE, CALIFORNIA.

LIFE LESSON #12: SET GOALS!

SEE WHY GOALS ARE CRITICAL TO YOUR SUCCESS IN THIS VIDEO.

Y ou have to make decisions in life about what it is you want! If you aren't clarifying your dreams and ambitions in a specific way, then you have no direction or pathway to help you pursue your dreams. Simply put, you won't know what to do until you know exactly what it is you want!

I spend time every week setting new goals for myself and reviewing and tweaking old goals. I've learned from experience that setting goals pushes one to achieve more, faster. When I force myself to strive for something that is out of my reach, it motivates me to take the appropriate actions to get there. Without goals in your life, you become content to settle for mediocrity, and you end up staying in your current state. Being stagnant is a killer! To get what you want in life, you have to be a mover and shaker, constantly taking action. Where you are at in your life right now isn't a reflection of your ultimate potential, but instead, it is the reflection of the goals you are choosing to focus on at this particular time.

When it comes to setting goals, it is vital that you set goals that inspire and motivate you! If you aren't inspired, you won't have the momentum to keep taking action to achieve your goal. Having a strong and powerful "why" you want something will drive you to the "how" to get there.

> **"SHOW ME A STORE CLERK WITH A GOAL, AND I'LL GIVE YOU A MAN WHO WILL MAKE HISTORY. BUT GIVE ME A MAN WITHOUT A GOAL, AND I'LL GIVE YOU A STORE CLERK."**
>
> —J. C. PENNY

Sometimes people are afraid to set goals because they've done so in the past and have not achieved them. They want to avoid the pain of failure they've previously experienced. But with each failure, you come one step closer to success! Don't allow your past to defeat your future. Most people stop and give up far too soon on their goals because they don't see the results right away. It doesn't work like that. To achieve anything great, it is going to take commitment and hard work.

It has been said that the common ingredient in nearly all successful people in the world is persistence. Successful people are persistent; they don't give up on their ultimate vision. Often, they have persevered through the bleakest of circumstances, but that undying tenacity paid off in the end. These types of people don't let things happen; they go out and make things happen the way they want them to be!

Does this mean if we write down our goals they just magically happen?

Of course not! Simply setting a goal does not make it happen. You must have a plan and then execute it! Remember: your life changes by action. There is, however, power in actually writing out your vision, and years of studies and testimonies validate this principle. Here are a few tips that I've learned from others that can help make your goal-setting the most effective it can possibly be. Most importantly, following this process will help you to start taking action!

WRITE IT OUT

There is something about actually writing your goals out on paper that makes them become more real. Writing down our goals can be an intimidating process and a huge step. Maybe you are embarrassed by your goal or scared of what other people will think of you. Writing down your goals is the first step in claiming them; you are telling the world, "This is what I want, regardless of what anyone else thinks."

FIRST PERSON AND DATE IT: BE SPECIFIC

Write your goals in first person format: "I, John, will lose 15 pounds by January 1 by changing my diet and doing hula dancing three times a week." The more specific you can be, the better. There needs to be some way you can measure your progress. Saying "I want to be in better shape" is too general and will prevent you from making progress.

Do you want to be able to run 5 miles at a 6:30/mile pace? Are you trying to fit back into your high school letterman jacket? Maybe you want to learn to speak Spanish. Whatever it is, be specific! That way you can measure your progress. Putting a date you will reach this goal by is critical. Maybe you want to buy a house in a certain area. But when do you want it by? In the next three months or five years down the line. Again, be specific! This puts you under pressure if you know there is a certain date you have to get it done by, which will motivate you to actually get it done! Having a completion date also gives you the ability to chart your progress and perhaps re-evaluate what is a realistic goal and what is not.

POST GOALS WHERE YOU CAN SEE THEM EVERY DAY

In order to achieve your goals, you need to make them a priority in your life. To make them a priority in your life, it is helpful to continually be reminded of them throughout the course of the day. That keeps you focused and committed to taking the actions necessary to get to where you want to be. Growing up, I kept my goals sheet in two places: hanging up in my locker at school and on my wall in my room. I had goals like graduating school with a 4.0 GPA, winning our basketball SE Alaska Championship, and getting my college education paid for by a basketball scholarship. The power of goal-setting helped me to achieve these things and more. Today, I still have my goals sheet on the wall by my bed.

"SUCCESS SEEMS TO BE LARGELY A MATTER OF HANGING ON AFTER OTHERS HAVE LET GO."

—WILLIAM FEATHER, PUBLISHER AND AUTHOR

You'll find that once you start achieving small goals, you'll start to dream bigger and bigger. Once these bigger dreams start becoming reality, it gives you the confidence to truly believe that the sky is the limit! Knocking out goals in my life has really taught me to believe in myself. Looking back, it's hard to believe I got to do some of the things I've done, and that has inspired me to dream even bigger! The sky truly is the limit! Remember, the biggest obstacle you'll ever have to overcome is yourself.

TELL OTHERS YOUR GOALS CONFIDENTLY

It is important to share your goals with other people. This can be frightening because, by nature, we tend to waste a lot of time worrying about what other people will think of us. Will they think I'm crazy and unrealistic? Are people going to judge me and talk negatively about me behind my back? Maybe they will. But what kind of life do you want to live? Do you really want to be like those who give up before they even get started for fear of what others think of them? You can't let your life be dictated by other people. Do what makes you happy and brings your life the most joy. You'll find that when you declare your aspirations confidently and with purpose, it helps you and those around you to believe in them. Believing is the first step. Go confidently in the direction of your dreams, and start living the life you've only imagined!

If you know the formula, it doesn't matter what the goal is, you can achieve it. Many use the excuse that they don't have enough time. Last time I checked, we all have the same 24 hours in a day. In all reality, everyone has the same amount of time. What these people actually lack is direction. You can hear the excuses all the time from those around us:

"I'll start training next month when I'm not as busy with school."

"Once the kids graduate and are out of the house we'll start traveling."

"Once the weather gets nicer we'll get on that project."

"After I get a raise, we'll start saving for our dream boat."

Newsflash! There is *never* going to be the perfect or right time to start taking action to get to where you want to be. You have to make it work and actively take steps in the right direction, despite whatever your circumstances at the time may be. Successful people don't wait around for the perfect time or season to make opportunities happen. Instead, they start making things happen in their current situations because they understand the importance of taking action and creating their own success.

Life is what we make it! Are you creating the life you want to live or going along with someone else's safe idea of your ideal life?

Setting goals can change your life forever. If you set ambitious goals, you are far less likely to suffer from depression because goals create a higher level

> ## "SETTING GOALS IS THE FIRST STEP IN TURNING THE INVISIBLE INTO THE VISIBLE."
>
> —TONY ROBBINS, LIFE COACH AND MOTIVATIONAL SPEAKER

of excitement in your life. This engaged activity helps you reach your objectives and provides inspiration. You should be setting goals for your career, family, fun, and how you want to help others. Maybe you want to donate money to an organization or volunteer at your local soup kitchen. Perhaps you want to take your family on the dream vacation, buy a yacht, or be the top salesman for your company. Whatever it is, every journey starts with a single step. Take that first step, and write your goals down TODAY. Then take action, and you will see the power and change it will evoke in your life. You may just find your life will never be the same.

Set goals.

2ND OVERTIME

INCREDIBLE PEOPLE AND OPPORTUNITIES

LIFE LESSON #13: SURROUND YOURSELF WITH PEOPLE YOU ADMIRE AND PEOPLE YOU CAN LEARN FROM

ver the course of my career, I've been lucky enough to meet some amazing people. Each time I interact with a successful person, I try to learn something from the way they live their life, and I think the lessons I've gathered will help you, too. When we take the chance to learn from the strengths of the people around us, we can use those lessons to propel our own lives in the direction of our dreams. In this chapter, you'll see the value of humility, hard work, and confidence, to name just a few principles. Success isn't about luck; it's about forming good habits and sticking to them as you pursue your dreams. As the expression goes: "The harder I work, the luckier I get!"

MS. HEIDI KLUM

eing an actor in L.A., I go out on auditions all the time. When you go out for a commercial audition, it's kind of a gamble, so you just have to go all out and hope for the best. You don't have time to worry about if you'll make a fool of yourself; you just have to be you. That's often how it is in life. Not many people get told "no" on a more regular basis than actors, even when we give it our all. But how you respond to rejection can make the difference between your success and failure. If you can begin to view rejection as a stepping stone that brings you closer to your next big break, it will inspire you to keep pushing forward, even when you aren't getting the results you want. Michael Jordan said,

"I'VE FAILED OVER AND OVER AND OVER AGAIN IN MY LIFE, AND THAT IS WHY I SUCCEED. I CAN ACCEPT FAILURE; EVERYONE FAILS AT SOMETHING. BUT I CAN'T ACCEPT NOT TRYING."

Using that life lesson, I've been able to perform in some really cool commercials because of my basketball ability, but when it's not basketball-related, it can be a bit tricky. They have you do the most ridiculous things at these auditions. I've had to kiss random girls after proposing to them, take my shirt off and be a sexy vampire while dribbling a basketball, and even learn a choreographed dance on the spot.

In the spring of 2013, I went out for a commercial that would turn out to be one of the funniest jobs I've had to date. I went in and was told I had to act like a pool boy who looks up and sees a hot "cougar" eyeing him from inside the house. The casting director proceeded to tell me that I had to then sit on the couch and act like the cougar was seducing me. He said "action" and some funny music came on, and I did my best to act out his odd instructions. I walked out of the room shaking my head. Was this real life? Other people were working at the bank or selling real estate. Not me. I was pretending to be seduced by an imaginary attractive older woman. It's moments like these when I realize how out-of-touch with reality life in the entertainment business can be. But what can you do?

I got the callback—which meant the casting director liked my audition and wanted me to come in again—and this time so that the director and ad agency could see me perform. I walked into the room with my hair slicked to the side and a little blazer on, and had six people staring at me . . . waiting for me to make them laugh. They had me do the same thing as the first audition. Again, I said my lines, did my best, and hoped they liked it. Then I was told they wanted me to seductively eat a burger for the camera. *What does that even mean?!?* I thought. This was one of those moments when I couldn't worry about looking stupid. I decided right then that I was going to go all in.

I took the biggest bite out of that thing as I could, batted my eyelashes, and then licked the burger up and down. It was definitely a little weird, but I wanted the part, needed the money, and figured, heck, what do I have to lose? I repeated my "sexy burger bite" a few times, and finally the director looked over to the others in the room and said, "Well, I don't know how we are going to do any better than that!" I stood up and said goodbye, and they thanked me for coming in. About ten minutes later, I got a call from my agent saying I needed to keep my schedule clear because they wanted to have the option to use me for the commercial. They confirmed that I'd landed the job later that day, and I was pumped, especially when they told me the big news: Heidi Klum would be playing the hot cougar who was going to seduce me! Talk about a great gig!

I was a little nervous on the day of the big shoot, but I've learned to tell myself that it's okay to be nervous. Nerves are a good thing and can help you perform at a higher level if you don't let them get to you. I've never played a basketball game I wasn't nervous about beforehand. The excitement and rush is what makes it so exciting! If you never leave your comfort zone, you'll never grow as a person. Once I came to this realization, it changed the way I approached my life dramatically. I used to avoid things that made me nervous and uncomfortable. Now, I push myself to do more things that scare me because I know it's good for me. It makes me grow as a person and gives me more confidence to do things that I wouldn't have before. If the thought of doing something scares you, you probably need to seriously consider doing it. Start stepping outside of your comfort zone more often. Whether it's speaking in public, asking that person you have a crush on for their number, or simply volunteering at a local soup kitchen, you may just find you like what happens to you as a result.

When I got to the set, they outfitted me for the part. Heidi came in glowing (I'm pretty sure there was a halo hanging over her head!), introduced herself to me, and was absolutely delightful. She was hilarious, joking around and singing funny songs, and we had a lot of laughs while shooting the scene. It didn't matter if you were the director or just someone who was there to clean up the garbage, Heidi took a sincere interest in everyone, which gave me so much respect for her. She even kept nominating random people on set to be given free lotto scratchers every time she saw someone hustling and going the extra mile with their work. Her caring spirit was a joy to be around and was contagious. She certainly possessed the 'likability factor' I've talked about. Heidi taught me a valuable lesson that day. By simply giving enthusiastic and genuine praise, you become more likable. If you take the time to start paying others sincere compliments, you'll find people will appreciate you more and be more prone to speak highly about you. Giving credit where credit is do is an easy way to win friends and influence more people.

She tried different "seduction options" on me (I wasn't mad about it one bit), and I tried not to feel uncomfortable. I'm pretty sure every guy on set that day wanted to switch places with me, but I wasn't going to let it happen! This was my moment, and I wasn't going to share it. I must have taken a bite out of at least a hundred burgers that day, but who's complaining? All in all, it was an exciting experience, and I got to show that I could do more than just dribble a basketball. My exposure from that commercial was awesome. Because of its "controversial" nature, it was featured on *The O'Reilly Factor* and *Good Morning America*, among others.

All over the world, guys want to know, "What was it like working with Heidi Klum?!"

I always smile and quietly say, "It was the best day of my life!"

To keep tabs on Heidi and see all the exciting things she is up to, as well as learn about all the ways she gives back to so many people, you can find out more at her website www.heidiklum.com and follow her on Twitter and Instagram here: @heidiklum

AND . . . IF YOU WANT TO SEE ME IN ACTION ON THE BEST DAY OF MY LIFE, HERE IT IS.

AND HERE'S THE BEHIND THE SCENES FOOTAGE!

THE TIME I WENT TO INDONESIA

AND BECAME BEST FRIENDS WITH ALLEN IVERSON (WELL, WE HUNG OUT A LITTLE BIT)

They were about to call my name. I was backstage, about to be introduced to thousands of fired-up streetball fans in Indonesia. The music was blaring, the MC was yelling into the mic, and everything was pitch black except for the spiraling spot light that was about to shine down on me. You could feel the pulse in the crowd growing with each word the announcer said, and I took one last deep breath to gather myself. That's when it hit me: I was about to take the court with one of the greatest basketball players of all time—Allen Iverson. I couldn't believe I was living this moment. Before

I could really take that thought in, the speakers rumbled: "Jesse . . . Spin Cycle . . . LeBeau!" It was my time to take the court.

I was visiting my family in Alaska when I got the call. I remember it well. We were out on our boat fishing, and it was a beautiful day. My phone rang, and it was my friend Pam from the streetball organization Ball Up. She asked me if I wanted to go to Indonesia and play in a big finale game with some of the best dunkers in the world. They were going to pay me and cover all of my expenses. Then she said the thing that changed everything, "Oh, and Allen Iverson is going to be your teammate. Do you wanna go?"

WHAT?! Umm . . . YES!!!

I hung up and looked at my mom and said, "I think I'm going to Indonesia to play with Allen Iverson." I was stunned and didn't know how to react. I didn't want to get too excited, just in case it fell through, so I tried my best to stay calm on the surface, but inside I was running around screaming like a little girl!

Fast forward a few months and it was time to ship out. I got to the airport half asleep for a red-eye flight to Taiwan, and there he was, Allen Iverson, getting on the plane right next to me. I didn't say anything and didn't want to bother him, but it was exciting to see him. I grew up watching him play, and the thought of spending some time with one of the most electrifying players in NBA history was a pretty exciting notion for me. AI changed the face of the NBA by bringing the way people were playing ball in the streets to the league. He has an incredible resume which includes being a #1 NBA draft choice, winning the Rookie of the Year Award, being an eleven-time NBA All-Star, and two-time All-Star MVP, winning the scoring title four times, and being second only to Michael Jordan with a playoff career scoring average of 29.7. He was exciting to watch with his lightning quick crossovers, fearless attitude, and willingness to do whatever it took to win, even if it meant nearly killing himself in the process.

IF YOU HAVEN'T WATCHED THIS TRIBUTE VIDEO TO ALLEN IVERSON, CHECK IT OUT. IT'S WORTH WATCHING SO YOU CAN SEE WHAT AN AMAZING PLAYER ALLEN IVERSON (AI) REALLY IS!

The fact that Allen was an underdog of sorts because he was "undersized"—only six feet—made him all the more appealing to me. I especially liked to watch his game because I could relate. He was doing the things that I had to do to be successful on the court against bigger competition. To see him do it on such a high level was nothing short of inspiring! All these things were going through my head as we boarded the plane for a faraway foreign land, and I drifted off to sleep wondering what the next few days had in store for me.

Nineteen or so hours later, I was in Jakarta, Indonesia, clearing customs. I had given AI his space and hadn't tried to talk to him; I didn't want to bother him because it was clear that most people did that. I've shared a little bit in this book about how I don't like to be very aggressive or pushy when I meet high profile people; instead, I would rather treat them as normally as possible. We are all just people, and it gets annoying when everybody always wants something from you or is acting like a "fan." I respected AI's space the best I could, and when we did interact I was the same person I always am—which basically means I talked a lot of trash (good-naturedly, of course). This usually throws people off at first, but they like it.

So at the airport, instead of crowding AI, I waited until he came up to me and introduced himself. He was really cool right off the bat. Taking his lead, I asked if he saw Rosario Dawson on our flight, and we shared a few laughs when I told him she was out of his league. He said he chatted with her for a little bit, and she was really nice; I definitely was a wee bit jealous. I was stuck in the back, crowded next to some smelly truck drivers, while he was up having witty conversations with a beautiful and talented actress. Allen 1, Jesse 0. The good thing was, it seemed like AI was going to be friendly and cool with me!

Boy, was this trip going to be a treat. We headed outside, where the cars were waiting to pick us up, and were immediately swarmed by media and fans with cameras. It was clear that I was with a star, and by default, I was going to be a star this weekend, too. I was a long way from the family fishing spot in Alaska!

Over the course of the next few days, I got to spend some good time with AI doing press, meet-and–greets, and just chilling out between events. One night, they prepared a huge spread of food for us, but AI showed up with a big bucket of KFC chicken, which I thought was hilarious. "I ain't taking no chances!" he said, dead serious, when we asked him about it.

Then the best thing *ever* happened: we started talking hoops. AI shared his perspective on the game, including first-hand stories about Michael Jordan and how different players reacted to his different moves. I was in basketball heaven! During the conversation, a few of the other players started talking about themselves, and I wanted to throw my shoe at them. *Let AI speak!* I wanted to hear those Michael Jordan stories! The really cool part was connecting one basketball player to another. I always talk about how basketball neutralizes the playing field with different people I meet. The same was true in this case. It didn't matter what color we were, where we grew up, or how much money we had. We all loved basketball. To see the light in AI's eyes as he told those stories was unreal; you could see him reliving big moments in his career from the all-star games to play-off runs, and I couldn't get enough of it!

I love to observe successful people. I watch how they interact with others and see how they think differently from other people. I enjoy learning the little things they do differently that separates them from the average person. I took away some very interesting insights from my time with AI, which I'll talk about in more detail later. More than anything, I was just surprised how approachable and kind he was to people that came up to him. You could tell he had a good heart and really appreciated his fans, which was cool because I was one of them!

HERE ARE A FEW PHOTOS FROM
ONE OF OUR PRESS INTERVIEWS.

AI seemed to take a liking to me, and he ended up talking to me quite a bit throughout the trip. My buddy showed up a few days late to play with us, and he was so confused and finally came up to me and asked, "Why does AI keep coming up and talking to you like you are best friends?'"

I laughed out loud and told him, "Because we are!"

We walked into this restaurant, and as if on cue, AI spotted us and came up smiling. "Hey, Jess, you are gonna love this spot!"

I gave my friend the look; he couldn't believe that we were on that level. I just smiled, feeling like the coolest kid in school, and I was loving every minute of it! That's how the joke of AI and I becoming best friends was born, and I am going to continue to stand behind the rumor for as long as I can!

One cool moment came after our game. We were out on the town having a good time and my group had to leave. I started walking to the door when I heard someone yell, "Hey, where you going? Stay and roll back with us." I looked back, and it was AI. "You down?"

In my head, I was screaming, "HECK YEAH, I AM!" but I managed to play it somewhat cool, and yelled to the others that I'd catch them back the hotel. We stayed a little longer, and it was worth it because on the twenty-five-minute car ride home we talked basketball and what it takes to be great.

He told me what he thought the difference was between some of these amazingly talented streetball players and most NBA players. He said players who wanted to be in the NBA had to have a better all-around game on both ends of the court and that is was crucial to be able to think the game, not just play it. He also shared the mentality and approach he felt you had to have to be successful in the game. He said, "You have to be tough, and you have to have confidence in yourself, even when your shots aren't falling." It was incredible being able to listen to him share his thoughts on the game of basketball with me.

I shared my opinions about the difference in players' mental toughness and asked him a few questions, and he asked me what I thought about what he had to say. I can't begin to describe how surreal this was. Allen Iverson wanted to know what I know what *I* thought. What dream world did I wake up in? I can't say it enough: it was *unbelievable* to be able to talk to someone, hooper to hooper, with so much experience at the highest level. I can't think of many times that were more enjoyable for me than this unique encounter with one of the greats.

At one point, he started talking me up, referring to some of the tricks I had done in the game, but I cut him off and basically said that basketball has been great to me, but "stop gassing me. I'm not NBA material. I'm too small, and I'm fine with that."

I'll never forget his reaction. He got real serious, looked back dead in my eyes, and said, "Don't ever say that again." I know he was just being nice, but it was cool to hear him say that, and after spending time with him, I can vouch that "The Answer" is a funny dude and a good guy! He's the type of person you just want to be around because he's going to find the humor in a situation. Plus, he's a good trash talker, and if you are anything like me, you need that in a friend!

HERE'S A PHOTO OF US BACK AT THE HOTEL AFTER TALKING ABOUT HOOPS AND LIFE ON THE DRIVE BACK HOME.

The actual game we played in was crazy! They packed this outdoor venue and had more lights and screens than a Jay-Z concert. They had smoke and DJs, along with dancers and performances out the wazzoo. This was a special game for me, not just because I was going to be taking the court with AI, but also because it was a chance for me to prove some things to myself. I wanted to push myself outside of my comfort zone. In a lot of these games I play in, I say I am going to do all these different trick moves, and then I usually do less than half of them. I believe this happens for several reasons: (1) I'm scared to look like I'm trying too hard and doing too much, and (2) the bigger chance you take, the bigger chance that something could go wrong and you'll embarrass yourself. So instead, I usually play it safe and then get mad at myself after the game. I was determined that I wasn't going to let this be the case this time. I was going to go for the slam dunk (literally and metaphorically) and just not care about what anyone thought or said. In my motivational presentations, I talk about principles like "Go All In" and "Take Action" and "Take 100 percent Ownership of Your Life." It was the time for me to put up or shut up! I was going to put on a show (sometimes known jokingly in my circle of friends as the "LeBeau Show") or crash down in flames trying!

And I did! AI held back during the game because he couldn't afford to get injured. I didn't mind; it gave me more opportunities to be the exciting play-maker. I went all out, from dancing like a fool in the introduction to doing some crazy moves and running into the crowd. The funny thing was, once I made the decision to go for it, I never looked back and had maybe the most fun I've had in my life playing basketball. Not everything went perfectly, but I wasn't afraid to fail, and that made all the difference. Like AI and I talked about later than night, your mindset can make all the difference. I experienced it firsthand that day. Not only did I get to take the court with a basketball legend that day and entertain a crowd,

> **"GO CONFIDENTLY IN THE DIRECTION OF YOUR DREAMS. LIVE THE LIFE YOU'VE IMAGINED."**
>
> —HENRY DAVID THOREAU, AMERICAN AUTHOR AND TRANCENDENTALIST

I got to prove to myself that when you apply these principles of success in your life, the reward far outweighs the risks. If I had given up on my dreams of basketball like I was supposed to, I would never have been able to travel to the other side of the globe and have this life changing experience with Allen Iverson.

CHECK OUT THE HIGHLIGHTS FROM MY TRIP WITH AI! (I AM THE LITTLE WHITE GUY; I GO BY "SPIN CYCLE" IN THE STREETBALL WORLD.)

I took away some powerful new lessons and reinforced some old principles from my amazing Indonesian experience with AI. Here are a few of them:

BE FEARLESS! BELIEVE IN YOURSELF!

One story that AI shared with me was his first time playing against Michael Jordan. He himself admits that he is a big Jordan fan, and he said that during warm-ups he kept looking down to the other end of the court because he'd never seen him in person before. But he told us that once the tip-off was thrown up, all his nerves went away, and it was just time to play basketball. I will never forget what he said next: "At the start of the game, everyone knew who Michael Jordan was. I was going to make sure that by the end of the game, they remembered who #3 was."

I about lost my mind when he said that! I love that mindset. Here he was, going up against the greatest player to ever play the game, and he had the attitude "I respect you, but today is my day to be the greatest." That is the winner's approach that is key to success in anything in life. You can't just hope for it; you have to claim it as fact. I've experienced radical changes in my performance on the court by merely adjusting my confidence level. I can dominate a game one day when I'm thinking that I am the best player on the court and no one can touch me. Then, the next game, I second-guess myself and play hesitantly, even timidly, and suck! I have the exact same amount of talent as I did in the previous game, but my mentality is weaker, and that changed the outcome of my performance. Take on the Michael Jordans in your life fearlessly, and I promise you will see results!

YOUR ATTITUDE AND MENTALITY ARE EVERYTHING!

Going along with the last point is knowing how to control your mentality and attitude. One thing that separates a lot of streetball players and NBA players is not their talent level, but rather what's going on in their heads! There's a good number of streetball players who are much more talented than NBA players, but because they have quick tempers, refuse to buy into a system, and make bad decisions in their personal lives, they will never play in the NBA.

There are going to be ups and downs in your career and life, no matter what you choose to do. AI battled all kinds of adversity, from chronic injuries to jealous teammates to disloyal friends, but he chose to persevere through it all. He possesses a true winner's attitude, and although he is amazingly talented physically, it is his tenacity and competitive fire that separates him as one of the greatest. There are many other players that can dribble just as well as he does, run as fast, and jump as high, and even higher. But nobody wanted it more. No one was going to exhaust every ounce of energy in their body and put it on the line like AI. His attitude and mentality made all the difference. The great part about that is we get to choose what our attitude/mentality will be every day. We can't control what happens to us, but we can control our response. Choose to be great, and choose to have a winner's attitude like AI!

DO WHAT YOU LOVE AND YOU CAN CHANGE THE WORLD!

One thing that I saw and was moved by was how touched people were in Indonesia when they talked about watching AI play. People would light up and share stories about watching this or that game or play-off run, and how he had made them want to play basketball. Here we were, about as far away as you can get from the United States, on one of the most remote corners of the earth, and people were impacted by someone they had never met. It's crazy how one person can change the lives of so many people, and it was powerful to see it firsthand. It inspired me to do what I love and become the best at it. And you can, too, because if you do, you can have a positive influence on an unlimited number of people. That's the kind of legacy I want to leave behind, one that matters and that makes a difference in the lives of others. I want to encourage you to take some time and think what this means for your life. What is it that you truly love? What's your mission in life? How can you help others and change the world? Do some soul searching, and find out what it is. Until you figure it out, you'll be living without purpose, and that will lead you to a very unfulfilling life.

SET BIG GOALS!

AI had goals to play in the NBA and be one of the greatest players to play the game. That's no little goal, by any means. Being undersized and battling less-than-ideal circumstances off the court, AI found that the odds weren't in his favor. But that didn't stop him. He battled though it all and came out on top.

I've found the same thing in my life. Sometimes setting big goals can be scary and intimidating. For example, going all out in that game was outside of my comfort zone. I'm sure there are things you would like to do but they are outside your comfort zone. I urge you to go for it! Remember this: everything you want in life is just outside your comfort zone. I learned that the day I took the leap of faith and went for it. I've also found that with every big goal I've achieved, the other goals that seemed so impossible and scary aren't as intimidating anymore. In fact, they seem very achievable and exciting. Learn from AI's example like I have. Set big goals, and don't hold back!

I may not be best friends with AI (but I might be . . . it's debatable), but I am so thankful that I got to have a fun trip and spend time on and off the court with him. This whole experience was a direct result of the principles I just listed above. You have to do what you love fearlessly, setting big goals, and you can change the world and live your dream life! I appreciate the lessons and insight I got from this special trip, and it will stick with me for as long as I live. I'll say it again, I'm the last person who should be getting to have experiences like these. I'm the undersized white kid from Alaska, remember? But by following these principles and playing by my own set of rules, I have set myself up for unique opportunities to do the things I love for a living. The choice is up to you. Think about this quote from one of my mentors, Dave Coates:

"THE HARDEST OBSTACLE YOU WILL EVER HAVE TO OVERCOME IS YOURSELF."

I'd like to give my appreciation to Ball Up, the streetball organization that has given me so many opportunities to travel, entertain, and be on TV playing the game I love with NBA players and celebrities. They have shown me nothing but love, and if you want to see some of the most talented and exciting basketball in the world, you have to check them out at www.ballupstreetball.com.

THE DAY I SHOT A "GANGSTA" RAP VIDEO WITH DR. DRE (AND AKON AND SNOOP DOGGY DOGGY DOGG)

I don't know how to put this delicately, so I'll just say it: I'm white. I'm sure that was a big shocker. Growing up in one of the whitest places in the world, Alaska, the last thing anyone would ever expect was for me to do is be in a music video with Dr. Dre.

As I've mentioned before, when I moved to L.A. to break into the entertainment business, I had no idea what I was doing. I was just following the "Go All

In" principle (see page #) and taking a leap of faith with the determination to learn as fast as I could as I went. Not having found my niche and thinking it would be beneficial, not to mention cool, to be in a rap video, I decided to go for it. Next thing I knew, I had been cast and was going to be in a club scene for a Dr. Dre music video entitled "Kush." My being in the shoot made about as much sense as letting Charlie Sheen babysit your kids. I didn't belong, and I certainly didn't pass the look test. Luckily, I was pretty used to that situation because of basketball background, so it didn't faze me at all. I showed up and was in some hot L.A. club with thug-looking dudes and some of the most gorgeous music video girls I'd ever seen. Dr. Dre, Akon, and Snoop Doggy Doggy Dogg were roaming around and talking with people, and I had to pinch myself a few times to make sure this wasn't some weird dream. It wasn't, and it makes for a great story that no one usually believes.

If someone took a picture of the scene that night and showed it to you, you'd point me out and be like, "That guy definitely doesn't belong in this picture. You'd say something to the extent of, "Someone did a really good job photoshopping this picture." Then you would probably show the picture to me, and I would agree with you.

But even though I felt out of place, I knew there were life lessons to be learned at the shoot. Besides having a lot of fun, I really hustled and did everything that I was told with a good attitude and to the best of my ability. I was surprised at how lazy the other people there were. They were there to do what I was doing, but it seemed like everyone was a complainer. They wanted to leave or fight over money, and the energy was so negative I didn't even want to be around it. It was 4 a.m., and I was tired, but to me, this was a once-in-a-lifetime opportunity, so I was eating it up. I was going to enjoy this opportunity and prove myself to be a hard worker. By doing so, they put me in a couple extra scenes. I've found that you can really impress people by going the extra mile and paying attention to the small details. So many people aren't willing to do that, and it's those little details that make all the difference. The funny thing is, going the extra mile doesn't usually require that much more effort. But the results you'll get can be truly rewarding and well worth the extra time and energy spent.

I remember watching Dr. Dre doing an interview very late into the night while everyone else was being lazy, trying to lay down, and coming up with an exit strategy. Not Dre, though. There was focus and intensity in his eyes and in his presence. At that moment, it became clear to me why this man was successful. It wasn't an accident. It wasn't the luck of the draw. He outworked everyone and wanted it the most. Here he was, a gazillionaire, famous, with millions of records sold, a guy who has every accolade you could ever want, and he was still up in the wee hours of the night perfecting his craft. Seeing him so focused inspired me that day. I never thought that would be my take-away from the experience, but I am thankful that I got to learn firsthand from the example of Dr. Dre. Nothing great was ever achieved or is worth achieving that doesn't require hard work. I try to copy the habits of people I admire, and Dr. Dre, as unorthodox as it may seem, is one of those people. I can already assure you he will continue to be successful because he approaches life with a winner's attitude, which is something we can all learn from. I like how Tiger Woods explained it:

"PEOPLE DON'T UNDERSTAND THAT WHEN I GREW UP, I WAS NEVER THE MOST TALENTED. I WAS NEVER THE BIGGEST. I WAS NEVER THE FASTEST. I CERTAINLY WAS NEVER THE STRONGEST. THE ONLY THING I HAD WAS MY WORK ETHIC, AND THAT'S BEEN WHAT HAS GOTTEN ME THIS FAR."

TO SEE ME IN THE MUSIC VIDEO, LOOK AT THE FOLLOWING LINK (FREEZE AT 1:45, 2:52, 3:13 TO SEE ME COMPLETELY OUT OF PLACE).*

*I do not condone the content of this video; in fact, it is so opposite of who I am, and I am so out of place it is actually quite funny.

A DAY WITH JUSTIN BIEBER

I get compared to "The Biebs" a lot. When I speak at schools, I always joke that I am a grown man trapped in the body type of Justin Bieber (minus the DUIs and bad tattoos, of course). When I found out I was going to get to be in one of his music videos, I'm not ashamed to admit that I was a little excited. Okay, I am a little ashamed . . . but I was more than a little exited. I mean, come on, we are talking about the Biebs here! Mr. Baby, Baby, Baby himself. Don't judge me.

The people at And1 Streetball called me up one day and told me they wanted to put me in a video with The Biebs. Honestly, I was just honored that the people at And1 knew who the heck I was. I'd always been an And1 fan growing up, so getting a call from them was really flattering. I agreed to do the job, so I hopped in an Uber (which I am absolutely obsessed with! Check them out; they will change your life: www.uber.com) and showed up on set not really sure what to expect. To my surprise, Busta Rhymes was also in the video, and I was told it would air as a promo for the start of the NBA season! This was turning out to be a pretty cool gig. I got a quick intro to The Biebs, and we started shooting. One of my favorite artists, Usher, came through to show JB some love, which automatically gave him about 10,000 more cool points in my book. Usher left, and then I got to watch The Biebs up close and personal, doing his thing in front of the camera, singing, playing the drums, and just being super charismatic and smooth. To be honest, I had never really paid much attention to his career prior to that point, but now I was blown away by how talented and full of "swagg" this guy was.

That was the day I became a Belieber. He is one confident dude, and I was impressed. Confidence and a strong belief can take you so far in life! I know I've experienced it on the court. One game when I believed in my ability I could completely dominate a game. Then, a few days later, if I was intimated or in my own head, I could totally suck. I had the exact same amount of talent in both games, but my own thinking had the power to dictate my results on the court dramatically. This principal carries over to your life and can play a huge role in your success or failure! A music artist like Justin Bieber is ridiculed daily on a massive scale all over the world from the things he says to the clothes he wears, even down to his haircut. If there is anyone who could become insecure and self-conscious, it's this guy! But he refuses to let others shape his own opinion of himself. He knows who he is and what he stands for. Know who you are, and love you for you. There's no one else out there like you! Attack your life with confidence, with your words and your actions, and you may just be surprised by the response you get back from the world.

After The Biebs shot a few scenes, I was handed a basketball and put on stage. Directors had me do some of my trick dribbling, cameras were zooming in and out from every direction while different colored lights flashed on me like I was at a rave. I've never been to a rave, but this is what I imagine it would feel like. It was awkward at first, and then I started to get in the rhythm and the butterflies went away; that's when it became a lot of fun. After they got the shots they needed, they brought The Biebs up on stage with me, and I became a backup dancer of sorts. We were both dribbling around and spinning the ball on our fingers without much input from the director. That is when I said my infamous line to The Biebs that almost ended my career . . .

Now let me give you a little backstory. I've had some very cool opportunities to spend time around celebrities, and I've always prided myself on not treating them any differently than any other person. It's a funny concept, this idea we have of "celebrity." I've seen people flock, scream, and faint when coming face-to-face with celebs and pro athletes. I've never really understood it, although it is quite fun to watch. At the end of the day, we are all just people who wake up in the morning and put our pants on the same way. I don't really see anyone as better than anyone else, despite how they choose to make a living. I've found that treating these "high profile" people like everybody else gets you a lot further with them. It gets old for them to have to answer the same questions, take pictures, and be approached by fans. Just by treating them like a regular person, and maybe talking a little smack (usually on the basketball court), I've been able to develop real, lasting friendships. People can tell when you have an agenda, so I try to be as genuine as possible. Sometimes though, I try to play it a little too cool, as was the case with Justin Bieber.

So there we were. Lights flashing, cameras on, music playing, and I turned to The Biebs between takes and asked him, "What are we supposed to be doing in this shot?"

He looked over at me, and cooly and casually replied, "I don't really know."

That's when it happened. I blanked. Maybe it was the heat of the cameras and lights, or maybe I didn't have enough to eat that morning, or maybe . . . this happens to everyone the moment they become a Belieber. I was tongue-twisted. The lights were on, but *nobody* was home. Drawing a blank, I awkwardly blurted out the first thing that popped into my head: "WHATEVER, BIEBS!"

That's when I knew The Biebs and I would never be friends, and he would probably hate me forever. Right then, I died inside. How could I sound like such a condescending jerk to the King of Cool, The Biebs himself?! I'd failed to treat him with the basic respect that every person deserves. I'd been rude, and I was wrong. What started off as such a promising day ended in complete shame. I knew I had let the LeBeau family name down, and I have been trying to redeem myself ever since.

It's been a long tough road, but I am proud to say I am almost fully recovered from my shameful incident. Every person deserves respect, and since that humbling experience, I've always tried to remember that principle. The hardest part is, for as long as I live, I will never be able to say anything to my family that they disagree with and not have them shout, "WHATEVER, BIEBS!"

I deserve it, so you laugh it up family; this one's on me!

MY THOUGHTS ON A DJ

'd like to share with you the story of a guy I look up to and have a great deal of respect for. His name is Scott Keeney, but most of you know him as DJ Skee. Recognized by *Forbes* and *Billboard* magazines as one of the most influential figures in the entertainment business today, Skee has created a unique lifestyle that is all his own, one that includes being heard daily on the radio by millions, hosting his own TV show, running a production company and record label, owning a retail store chain, and performing with some of the biggest stars all over the world. Recently, Mark Cuban called him the "Oprah of hip hop." This is just the tip of the iceberg, but in short, Skee does it all. He is a modern day renaissance man, if you will.

I've had the privilege to meet him a few times, twice at his infamous Skee Lodge during events and during the taping of his show across from the Staples

Center. With every encounter, I was very impressed by his humility and fascinated by his story. After a bit more research, I became even more inspired by his journey to the top. He is someone who truly embodies taking action and creating his own success. He takes complete ownership for his life, isn't afraid to fail, and 100 percent commits to his decisions. His work ethic is unrivaled. It seems he figured out early on that you can't hire someone else to do your pushups.

At age sixteen, Skee got into music. He was introduced to a well-known radio DJ in New York and saved his money to fly out there from Minnesota so he could learn how the music industry worked. He got to be around guys like Redman and Cam'ron and hustled to make the most of every opportunity. When Skee returned home to school, he sold mixtapes to his classmates (as well as rare sneakers and video-game consoles), and even cold-called record stores to sell them his mixes. Back then, the CD burners were so slow that he would set his alarm for every hour so he could burn a new CD on the hour. Talk about a hustler!

As fate (or the laws of attraction) would have it, Skee created a way to meet Steve Rifkind, the founder of Loud Records. At the time, Rifkind was in a desperate search for a PlayStation2 for his son for Christmas. Skee, being proactive and resourceful, got creative and got his hands on a PS2, but would only give it to Rifkind if he could do it in person. Upon delivery, Skee pitched Rifkind several ideas that could improve his company. Here he was, a high school kid, telling a successful business owner how he could make his company better. Talk about confidence! Rifkind was so impressed with Skee's effort and ambition that he decided to take him under his wing. This was a huge break for Skee, and he maximized it to the fullest.

Skee, realizing he had a huge opportunity on his hands, decided to go all in and take the leap of faith. He worked his tail off, graduated high school a year early, and moved to L.A. on his own to work for Rifkind. He learned on the fly and quickly impressed Rifkind with his drive and dedication. Before long, he had worked his way up to top accounts with Chrysler and T-Mobile.

Fast forward to the present day, and Skee is at the forefront of popular culture. He is the voice of a huge satellite radio program and the face of a TV show, runs top marketing campaigns, remixes songs with the world's biggest artists, provides content that plays in places like McDonald's, Taco Bell and Denny's, travels the globe speaking, hosting, and performing, and of course incorporates his love of sports and sneakers into almost everything he does. He has access to nearly anyone on the planet he wants to reach, and rightfully so. He's worked his butt off and created his own luck to live a life of his own choosing.

What I love about Skee's story is that he embraced nearly every success principle we touch on in this book. He found his purpose (sharing music and pop culture stories with others), went all in by saving up money to fly to New York and graduating from high school a year early so he could move to LA. Leap, and the net will appear! From day one, he took complete ownership of his life and didn't expect anyone else to make it happen for him.

Some people probably thought, what does a white kid from Minnesota know about hip hop? There were a million obstacles for him breaking into the industry, but he chose not let them stop him. I mean the kid was willing to wake up every hour on the hour just so he could burn CDs to sell to his classmates! Talk about living a life with no excuses! He then surrounded himself with people who were older, smarter, and more well-connected than himself. He took action and worked tirelessly to work his way up the food chain to become respected and well known. There is no substitute for hard work. Through it all and to this day, despite all his success, he continues to remain humble and let his work do the talking for him (except for when his work is to talk, which happens to be a lot of the time). DJ Skee is the quintessential American success story and a shining example that if you work hard enough and believe in yourself, anything is possible!

You can follow DJ Skee on Twitter and Instagram at @DJSkee. To learn more about DJ Skee, or to see where and when you can find him on radio, TV, and the Internet, visit www.djskee.com

"THE PROFESSOR"

I will always be grateful for the opportunities I have had to meet and become involved with many great people because of basketball. One of those great people is Grayson Boucher, or as many people know him, "The Professor." Fess was one of the original And1 Streetball players that toured the nation and was televised on ESPN. Streetball became a huge trend all over the world, and although it has recently slowed down in the US, it is still immensely popular overseas. I used to watch these guys play when I was in high school, and I was blown away by their moves and their style of play. Few of us had ever seen some of the moves and dunks these guys were doing! Fess became well known throughout the world for his precision dribbling skills and his flair for the theatrics. Being undersized and white, he also won over a lot of crowds by sheer shock factor. Surprised fans never expected a little white boy to be able to play at such a high level with bigger and stronger opponents, and especially not to embarrass them the way he usually did.

A carryover of the Fess's fame rubbed off on me starting in 2005. At pretty much any gym I played in, people called me "The Professor" or "White Chocolate." Although I found it annoying at first, after a while, I definitely took it as a compliment.

Fast forward a few years . . . The Professor and I were in San Diego doing a video shoot for a sports accessory watch company called Deuce Brand. It was a lot of fun, and I had a good time meeting and getting to know Fess on the shoot. He is a great guy, an amazing basketball player, and a kind, genuine person.

However, when we were first getting to know each other, he had every reason not to like me. I was basically another young version of him coming up in the game, and I was starting to make a little bit of a name for myself in the basketball/commercial world. At some point on the day of the shoot, we decided to play a game of 2-on-2 on an outdoor court at South Mission Beach. What started out as a fun little game out on the beach quickly turned into two little white guys battling it out for supreme bragging rights! My team, comprised of me and a random player I met at the beach, won the first game, and I could see the dynamic change almost instantly. It was on! All our competitive juices were flowing and in full effect! Not being one to back down, especially from the player I had constantly been compared to, I rose to the challenge, and the plays started to get more and more physical. Before I knew it, we were scratching and banging, and I was bleeding.

I remember having the thought, *Why? What is the point of this? What am I trying to prove?"* I admired Fess and was far more interested in developing a friendship with him than winning a random pickup game! As the game continued, it was getting rough, rough to the point that somebody was probably going to come out injured. So I made a choice. It was a hard choice for me and my competitive nature. I chose to back down. It wasn't worth throwing a guy to the ground to fulfill my ego, if that's what it took to win in this situation.

Although I only made a slight alteration in the way I was playing, it was enough to cost us the game. That stung, but when I looked past that minor irritation, I knew I had something which mattered to me more: the beginning of a friendship. It has been pretty cool to call someone I look up to, like 'The Professor', my friend. It isn't always about winning and doing whatever it takes to win. Sometimes, it about being able to feel good about the effort you made and the skills you gained. I've found that, in certain cases, you have to check your ego at the door and trust your gut. Being competitive is a great quality, but sometimes it can get you in trouble if you don't keep the big picture in mind.

Ironically, part of me wished I hadn't backed down that day. Now that I know him better, I'm convinced that Fess wouldn't have stayed mad over our battle if he hadn't come out on top. If anything, he would have respected me more. He's a competitor just like I am, and he isn't threatened by other people's success. In fact, he is a huge encourager and celebrates the success and victories of those around him. I've always believed that there is enough success to go around for everyone. Another person's success doesn't mean our failure, or that there will be less opportunity for us. It's easy to get jealous of others, and I've been on both ends of it. John F. Kennedy said, "A rising tide lifts all the boats." Of course, he meant it about the economy, but it applies here as well. The successes of the people around you in your field can lead to increased opportunities for you. Learn to be sincerely happy for others when they succeed; your big break could be next! Fess is an awesome example of what every athlete should represent. He is a great basketball player, and an even better person. But know this, Fess, I'm ready for my two-on-two rematch, and I'm coming for you next time! I won't be backing down!

Fess still travels all over the world, entertaining crowds with the streetball company Ball Up. He is an amazing example of someone who has created a unique lifestyle all his own doing what he loves to do. Despite many major obstacles that could have easily been excuses for him to give up, he persevered. His belief in himself and his dreams has created an awesome reality that has allowed him to see far-off places across the globe and continue to play basketball to this day. Another big element to his success has been his work ethic. Fess is a fellow little Frenchman, so I respect how much time Fess put into practicing and becoming the great player he is today. Unlike many of the guys who are born with the crazy ability to jump and don't have to work for it, Fess had to put in countless hours to be able to do the things he does today. He is living proof that if you work hard and believe in yourself, anything is possible!

Another quality I admire about Fess is that he uses his platform to encourage and give back to others. To me, that's what it is all about. With every decision we make, we are deciding who we are going to be. Fess continues to be a great basketball player and has proven to be an even better person, one I look up to a great deal. To stay up-to-date on his world travels, games, and videos follow him on Twitter at @professor12 and on Instagram at @globalhooper.

Find out lots more on his website www.graysonboucher.net

ROB DYRDEK AND THE FANTASY FACTORY

t's no secret. Even though I would break every bone in my body if I tried to skateboard, I'm still a huge fan of pro skateboarder and reality TV star Rob Dyrdek. I've watched all his shows, from *Rob and Big* to *Fantasy Factory* to *Ridiculousness*. I think Rob is hilarious! He's also a business genius, and has a huge heart. He is always giving back. I look at what he's done, and I'm inspired to create an empire like he has. He wakes up every morning and loves what he does, then uses his success to help others. Plus, I always knew the guy would be a blast to hang out with! When I got the opportunity to go to the one and only Fantasy Factory, it would be an understatement to say I was stoked out of my mind!

There was a big boxing match being televised, and Rob was having some people over to watch it. Although I'm not much of a boxing fan, I was invited, so I went to check out the Fantasy Factory. I rolled over there with a couple of buddies (in an Uber, of course), and when we walked in . . . it was everything you'd imagine it to be! Basketball hoops, half pipes, foam pits, a donkey for the animal lovers to pet, and lots of beautiful ladies. I got a chance to meet Rob and talk to him for a quick second. He was such a nice guy and came off very humble, which is something that always impresses me when I meet very successful people. To have it all and be on top of the world, yet not be full of yourself, is a rare thing, and that quality probably helped propel him to the top. I really respect that attitude when I see it. I thanked him for having us over to The Factory, and he was very kind and engaging. He didn't have to waste his time on me; I was nobody to him. There were a hundred other more exciting things he could be doing, like foam pit diving, petting donkeys, or shooting tennis balls at people. But he took the time to take an interest in me, and I appreciate him for doing so. It's funny how much of an impact we can make on others by simply taking a genuine interest in them, just as Rob did with me that day. Rob's example is one we all could learn from.

All in all, we had a good time watching the fight, and the night ended with a great surprise! Since there was a basketball hoop at the Factory, we ended up on the court. Before I knew it, I was playing in a heated game with my friends against Rudy Gay of the Sacramento Kings and a couple of his teammates . . . in front of everyone. We started to put on a little show, doing some fancy streetball maneuvers and throwing lobs to the big guys. My buddy, Chris Brew, really got the crowd going with his dunks. There was a weird moment when the thought popped into my head: *Am I really playing in front of a crowd at the Fantasy Factory against NBA players? Somebody pinch me because this isn't really happening!*

The more you dream big and just go for it, the more exciting doors will open up for you. That which most perceived as impossible has become part of my reality! That can happen for you, too! I'm the last person who should be having these exciting random experiences, but basketball and following my dreams have made it happen. With each new experience, you will believe in yourself more and more, and you'll see that any success is well within your reach.

ROB DYRDEK, PART 2: THE DAY I ALMOST KILLED ROB

As fate would have it, I got to spend some more time at The Fantasy Factory. I got a call while I was out in New Orleans (doing the Uncle Drew Campaign for NBA All-Star weekend with Kyrie Irving, which was a blast!) that when I got back I was going to be shooting a commercial at The Factory with Rob. I was stoked! At the time, all I knew was that I would be doing something with basketball. The day of the shoot came, and I was quickly shuffled onto set. It was circus! Almost every crazy scenario you could think of was going on that day. They had people juggling fire, a sumo wrestler, a human bowling ball knocking over pins, unicyclists, random animals walking around, and even a falcon—it was nuts! I was enjoying the freak show when the director came up and said to me, "Are you ready for the bear?" to which I replied, "What?" He continued saying, "Oh, yeah, we got a live bear, a grizzly actually. They are about to bring him in. If you have any food in your pockets, you should throw it away. Oh, and don't take any pictures. The flash can trigger the bear to attack." I did not know that this was what I signed up for, and I was shocked; my face said it all. The director looked at me and said, "Yeah, Rob is going to high-five the bear." Unfortunately for me, what I heard was, "Your job is going to be high-fiving the bear." I freaked!

I started pacing around, sweating profusely, and asking myself, "Why me? What did I do to deserve this punishment? I'm too young to die, and this isn't the way I wanted to go!" I was in full panic mode, and after my little freak-out session, they asked me what was wrong, and I said I didn't want to high-five the grizzly bear. They laughed at me and explained that Rob was the one who was going to be up close and personal with the bear, and I could relax. I wish the story ended there, but it doesn't.

They brought the bear in, and everyone was really on edge. Was this grizzly going to eat Rob or would everything be okay? The trainer slowly led the bear in, and we all watched in eager anticipation to see what would happen. Rob extended his hand, and we all held our breath and waited. To our delight, the bear gave him an impressive high-five! It was maybe one of the coolest things I've ever seen. That's when I had the thought that I think any normal person would have: *There is no way I'm not getting a picture of this on my phone.* So I slyly pulled it out, made sure the flash was off, held it up, and snapped my money shot.

BOOM!

The biggest flash in the history of flashes went off; it was like a lightning bolt had hit the inside of the fantasy factory. It was one of those movie moments where something awkward happens and the DJ stops the music abruptly and everybody stares at the perpetrator. Everyone's head jerked my direction, eyes wide, and then quickly back to the bear to see what he would do. Even the bear looked back over his shoulder at me! Then we waited. It was a scary moment. Thankfully, there was not a bear attack that day, and Rob wasn't harmed in any way. I was chewed out and in big trouble, as I should have been. I was just happy that I wasn't going to have to read headlines like, "Idiot Kills Rob Dyrdek in Tragic Bear Incident." The takeaway from this experience for me was follow the rules or else you could get someone eaten by a bear because you are an idiot who doesn't know how to work an iPhone! They make rules for a reason, and I should have followed them. There could have been serious and deadly consequences for not following protocol, but luckily, this time we just have this funny story and everyone was okay. To check out the infamous picture I took, as well as a shot of Rob and I, see below.

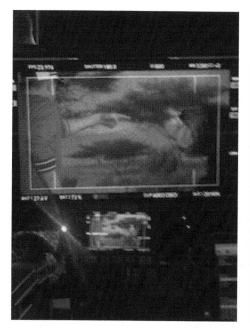

MY INFAMOUS PICTURE.   ME AND ROB DYRDEK ON THE SET.

WHAT I'VE LEARNED FROM STERLING BRIM

ne of the funniest people I know is my friend Sterling Brim a.k.a. Steelo. You may know him as Rob Dyrdek's co-host on the MTV shows *Ridiculousness* and *Fantasy Factory*. Sterling is a prime example of someone who has embraced a few different success principles and created an awesome brand and life that allows him to do the things he loves to do for a living. Here are a few of the principles I've seen him apply to his life, along with hard work, that helped lead him to the land of opportunity.

Sterling surroundeds himself with great people, like Rob and the rest of the Fantasy Factory crew. I can't think of many people who are more successful, not to mention fun, to have in your inner circle of friends. Those guys have a blast doing some of the most daredevil stunts you can think of, hosting and producing fun and hilarious shows,, and giving back by helping a lot of underprivileged kids. By keeping solid people in his life, Steelo's has had the opportunity to star on TV shows, build a strong brand, and even create a clothing line. They say you are the average of the five people you spend the most time with. This applies to how much money you make, where you are at in your career, how successful you are in school, your relationships with your family and romantic partner, and so on and so forth. Sterling is a great example of how you should surround yourself with motivated, good-hearted people.

The second thing Sterling has going for him is his overall likability. He's enjoyable to be around, he's funny, and he isn't afraid to make fun of himself. People are naturally attracted to him because he's so positive and exciting. Being likable is one of the most consistent qualities I've found in people who are successful. Nobody wants to be around a pessimistic grump!

Lastly, Sterling stands up for what he believes. I admire this quality in people because it's hard to do. It's what true leaders do, and more of us could be better at it. If you've watched him on his shows, or spent any time around him in person (or know anyone who has), you know Sterling isn't afraid to speak his mind, no matter how controversial the topic may be. Even if you don't agree with him, you have to respect someone who boldly states their views and doesn't back down from what they truly believe in. As the saying goes, "Stand for something, or you'll fall for anything."

These are just a few of the things I've taken away from my time with Sterling. I try to learn from others who are successful, and I think we all can benefit from his example.

TO LEARN MORE ABOUT STERLING, YOU CAN CHECK HIM OUT @ STEELOBRIM ON TWITTER AND FIND HIS FASHION LINE HERE.

JOHN BENDHEIM

asketball has gotten my foot in the preverbal door time and time again! It amazes me how many opportunities have come my way because of it. In the summer of 2013, I spoke to the Junior Achievement Board of Directors in L.A. and was able to connect with some powerful people at this first class organization. One of the board members contacted me after our meeting and said they were impressed with my Fab4 Takeover program and wanted me to go meet with a powerful friend of theirs. I said, "Awesome. Let's do it!"

When I looked up who the "friend" was, I could see I was in way over my head. This guy was on the Forbes list of wealthy and powerful people in the United States, and he was involved with so many major things it was like he was running the city of Los Angeles! How was some kid going to connect with a top business mind in the world? What would we even talk about? All I know how to do is dribble a basketball, so why would this guy even care to give me any of his valuable time? Those were some of my first thoughts, but I quickly forced myself to think more positively and see what this meeting might bring. I got my pitch together and headed to his office. I got there just early enough to listen to him ream some guy out for not being a good leader. If this was how he spoke to another adult, I couldn't imagine the type of conversation we were about to have!

Walking into his office felt like a scene out of a movie. There was signed sports memorabilia everywhere from top athletes and photos of John with everyone short of the Dali Lama himself! We had a pleasant conversation, and before I knew it, John insisted I show him some of my basketball skills and tricks. To add to the pressure, he began calling people into his office to watch! I tried to shut it down, but he was persistent. He took a basketball, signed by Phil Jackson, out of a glass case that also contained a photo of him and Phil in it, and threw the ball at me.

"Alright, show us something."

Was this even real life? Here I was with this incredibly powerful and influential guy, who I had just met—someone I should have no business even talking to—and yet now he trusted me enough to ask me to dribble an autographed ball around his office! What made it all possible? Basketball. The thing I was always told I was too small to do . . .

Truth be told, I was terrified I would break something in his office. It all looked really expensive, and I'm sure it was. But I looked around, took a deep breath, and went for it! All out, holding nothing back. I nailed my routine, and they loved it! I got what I needed from that meeting, and developed a relationship with a man who could put me in front of opportunities I never even knew existed before I met him.

Embrace your gift and perfect it. Use it to set you apart from the competition. Be the best, and people will remember you for it. I get paid to speak and mess around with a basketball for a living—how cool is that? What are you passionate about? What do you love so much that you would do it for free? The key to life, in my opinion, is to get so good at that thing that you get paid to do it! I challenge you to find that passion in your own life, perfect it, and use it to do something great!

ELIZABETH STANTON'S GREAT BIG WORLD

n the fall of 2013, I began working on a project that I am really excited about: an episode of "Elizabeth Stanton's Great Big World!" on FOX. I met Elizabeth at an event I attended with my friend Taylor. Taylor gets invited to a lot of events because he is an awesome and successful actor. Bless his heart, he invites me to some fun events with cool people.

We made quite an entrance at one particular event, which was the first evening of an entire weekend planned for celebrity attendees. We didn't know that it was going to be a big, classy dinner, and we showed up late. Imagine a Ritz Carleton-esque lavish dinner with a bunch of folks dolled up in their finest ballroom attire. There was fine wines, classy music, and an proper, middle-aged crowd. Now visualize the late entrance of two raggedy kids who looked like they'd just finished playing basketball and hadn't showered. That was our grand entrance to this tasteful night of charity.

When we walked in, it became obvious that we weren't properly attired, but we said the heck with it, we were hungry! People were staring at us, and you could see what they were thinking: "These kids are clearly lost." Security actually came up to us and asked us to leave. Luckily we were able to tell them who we were and that we were invited guests. They were embarrassed and apologized, and they let us in, and more importantly, we got our food! I'll never forget as we were walking around and people were giving us funny looks, Taylor tapped me on the shoulder and asked, "Is that Alex Trebek?" Indeed it was! We certainly weren't prepared for such a night and had to laugh about it. We ended up driving 45 minutes away and buying new clothes for the rest of our three-day stay.

We may not have made the smoothest entrance or known what we were supposed to wear, but we took action to be there and figured it out as we went. I've found that that is a great way to attack life! If you want something, go get it! It's easy to find an excuse and come up with a hundred reasons why you shouldn't do something right now. It's important to do your research and make smart decisions, but at some point, an opportunity will come along, and if you don't take action, someone else will, and that chance you had will be gone forever. Don't be someone who sits on the sidelines their whole life. Get out there and take action; it's the only way you are ever going to accomplish anything!

Taylor and I had a blast that weekend, and most importantly, we met our close friend to this day, Elizabeth Stanton. Besides being a hilarious, awesome person from a great family, "Lizzy" has one of the best educational programs on TV. She has passion, and that has made her show extremely successful. She takes her friends to exotic places all over the world and gives viewers a taste of how people there live. Her show really opens young peoples' eyes, helping them realize how blessed they are to have the luxuries of freedom, running water, and electricity. Lizzy really makes a difference and is passionate about it!

Right now we are working on an episode that will feature my Fab4 Takeover program. It will show the Fab4 Team going into an underprivileged area to a low-income school where we will make a difference. My team of players consists of my different friends on TV shows and some of the top basketball entertainers in the world. We come together and teach kids in the classroom with the help of Junior Achievement. After we do that, we hold an assembly and put on a basketball show for the school. Included in the package we present is the sports entertainment and a segment where we speak to the kids about bullying, leadership, and motivation. This is what I am passionate about, and it is the legacy I want to leave behind. The Fab4 Takeover has a couple of the best slam dunkers in the world on our team, plus an ex-NBA player, an author who played ball at Kentucky, and a basketball dribbling specialist who puts me to shame! We put on an incredible show that really impacts youth, and I am excited to have Lizzy be a part of it. Being on her show will give us amazing exposure and hopefully allow us to go to more schools to make a difference in the lives of so many young people. Lizzy has a big heart, and I am thankful to her for letting The Fab4 use her platform to help other people.

CONCLUSION

I had a baseball coach who once told me you have to be like a sponge in life. You have to continually absorb all the wisdom you can from others. You will never stop learning; it's a continual process. If you ever think you've reached the point where you think you know it all, you are in trouble, and you need a serious attitude adjustment! I've been blessed to spend time around some incredible people. With each opportunity, I try to take something away that can benefit my life and help me be more successful. I hope the lessons I shared in the stories in this chapter will add value to your life and help you to see every person you encounter as an opportunity to grow and learn. You don't have to be around famous celebrities to do this; you can learn something from nearly everyone you come in contact with! The key is to surround yourself with great people who are successful, positive, and want to see you be great. You are the average of the five people you surround yourself with, so choose wisely!

Surround yourself with incredible people.

LIFE LESSON #14: CHANGE YOUR SPHERE OF INFLUENCE!

LEARN WHY THE PEOPLE YOU SURROUND YOURSELF WITH PLAY A
KEY ROLE IN YOUR SUCCESS IN LIFE IN THIS VIDEO!

You've probably heard the saying, "Show me your friends, and I'll show you who you are." Studies have shown that you are the average of your five closest friends. Scary? It can be; maybe it's time to re-evaluate who you are choosing to spend your time with. Choosing friends isn't easy. Some friends are forced upon us by our parents, our significant others, or even the places where we work or go to school. But at the end of the day, we each have the ability to decide who we are going to call our closest friends.

Growing up immersed in the basketball world, I applied this principle to my life at a very early age. Although I was smaller than the rest of the kids my age, my coordination, speed, and skills developed much earlier. At the age of nine, I was dribbling through my legs and around the back in games better than some kids at our local high school. It was clear that I wasn't going to get better playing against my peers. I knew I had to surround myself with players who were better than me so I could improve.

So in the fourth grade, I went to our new recreation center and started playing against the adults. It wasn't easy to convince them to let me play at first, but luckily, I had a close friend who was about 6'6" named John Urbania, who made sure they let me play. Obviously, the adults at the gym were bigger, faster, stronger, and just overall better than me at basketball. At first it was frustrating, and they wanted to take it easy on me. When my older brother came around, he demanded that they steal it from me or block me whenever they could. He knew and helped me realize that the only way to get better was to get my butt kicked, forcing me to have the desire to not let it happen again. Strangely enough, he was right! I learned how to shield the ball from bigger and stronger defenders, how to create space to get my shot off, and how to have a quicker release. As time went on, I was able to hold my own as a youngster and then, eventually, out-play them.

If I would have continued to play with my classmates, I wouldn't have faced people who were better than me and been pushed to become better myself. I completely believe that the success I experienced in my basketball career came from competing with more talented players who gave me a fire in my belly to want to be better than them. Learning that I had to play with better people than me at an early age taught me the importance of this principle, and I have worked hard to apply it to other areas of my life. I was always determined to achieve my dreams, no matter what anyone else said or thought. Choosing to do the things that would make me consistently better is a huge reason I've gotten to where I am today.

Just as you should surround yourself with people who are more talented than you are, surround yourself with people that are more intelligent and savvy that you are.

In high school, I knew I needed to get good grades in order to get into a good college. I started to spend time with the smart kids who wanted to get straight A's just like I did. I chose to work with them on group projects, study guides, and other assignments. Doing well in school then became fun, and this made it much easier for me to succeed and graduate with a 4.0 GPA.

After college, when I blindly came out to Hollywood, I knew I had no clue about how the entertainment business worked. I knew I had some basketball skills, a lively personality, and more drive than the next guy, though, so I decided to use the gifts God gave me to surround myself with people who were more knowledgeable and talented people in the business. I found out where the big actors, directors, and producers played ball, and I went to learn from them. I came in without an agenda; I didn't ask anybody for anything, and I played ball, being my usual outgoing, upbeat self. I quickly made friends, and opportunities opened up for me not long after. I never missed an opportunity to play ball with this group of people. I attended the open gyms like it was my job because I was serious about surrounding myself with successful people who were further along in their careers than I was. There was no need to reinvent the wheel; I just knew I could learn from people who had already succeeded in what I was trying to achieve.

On the basketball court, they looked up to me and were excited about the way I played the game, so it allowed me to approach new people who I'd only seen on TV not as a fan, but as an equal. Sometimes being more skilled almost gave me the upper hand as I became a more valuable player that people wanted to have on their team. Because of this, basketball has been a beautiful place for me to network and build relationships with great people who are better and smarter than me. The side benefit is that it has helped me get better and smarter, as well!

Find people who are already successful doing whatever it is you want to do, and study them! Pick their brains! Become their friends! When you start to surround yourself with others who are focused and like-minded, you'll find that your way of thinking changes; you tweak your lens, and you start seeing things from a new perspective.

Once I met some different people who were doing well in the commercial industry, I learned a lot of things in a hurry. I discovered I needed an agent, so I went out and got one. I saw that I could benefit from taking different classes (which I did), and I slowly began to gain valuable insight on the ins and outs of the business. I was told I needed headshots to submit at auditions, and so I went to a photographer and had those taken. I closely watched what the guys who booked the most jobs did at their auditions, and I applied it to my approach. I also paid attention to those who weren't booking and made sure I didn't make the same mistakes. Whatever your craft is, whatever it is you aspire to do or be, you have to take it seriously, as if it is already your job, even if it isn't yet.

Expand your relationships with good people who will help you reach your goals. I learned from my associations that the players and actors who booked the most gigs all had something special they brought to the table. Some were seven feet tall, others could jump fifty inches high and dunk over people, and some were just really good at looking like a stereotypical basketball player. But I saw my "weaknesses" as my strength. Nobody was going to be able to be a better Jesse LeBeau than me! I looked really young, I was white, and I could dribble a basketball and do tricks that no one else could do. That was the one thing I could work on to ensure my highest chances of success, so that's what I did! I was determined to become an expert trick artist with the basketball, and it still helps me get my foot in all kinds of doors to this day.

Equally important to making great friendships is to limit (or even eliminate) people who are taking value from your life. We all know people who are negative. Many times they can be some of the people we are closest to. Distance yourself from these people and their baloney! Don't let a loser's mentality infiltrate your thinking. These people will say things like, "You need to go get a real job" or "You aren't smart enough to start your own business." As hard as it may be, it is critical for you to keep away from such negativity and the people who provide it. How much more energized do you think you will become if you have people saying positive, encouraging things to you on a regular basis? You are what you think. If you can continue to believe in yourself, and visualize reaching your goals, you'll be that much closer to actually seeing those goals become reality!

The brain is a very powerful organ, especially when you harness the power of positive self-thought. It can be difficult to tell someone you've known for years that you can't continue the relationship if it is toxic to you reaching your goals. But if you are serious about getting to where you want to be, you have to cut out negativity and surround yourself with positive people and positive thinking.

Change your sphere of influence.

HERE'S A GREAT TALK ABOUT THIS TOPIC.

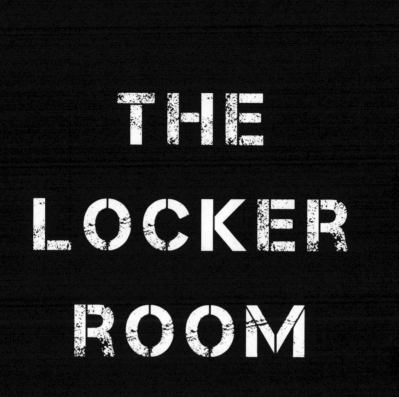

THE LOCKER ROOM

THE POST-GAME

REFLECTION

t's amazing how anyone can take life by the horns and truly create a dream life.

My dream life: getting paid to play basketball and help other people in the process! Although I was born with the opposite genetic prototype for a basketball player, I'm amazed at how hard work and believing in myself has gotten me so far down the road to my dreams. Through basketball, I've been able to:

- Get my college education paid for.
- Pay my bills without working a conventional nine-to-five job.
- Travel the world and be coached by guys like Chauncey Billups, Matt Barnes, Tyreke Evans, and Dennis Rodman.
- Have fans that look up to me, giving me the opportunity to be a role model.
- Play in internationally televised games against people I grew up watching on TV.
- Star in a Kobe Bryant commercial and in other commercials with the most recognizable athletes in the world.
- Be in a movie with Kevin Durant!
- Become a card-carrying member of SAG (Screen Actors Guild), because my "basketball-handling ability" is considered a special skill in the industry.
- Make unbelievable friends who are famous, have platforms, and can influence others for good!
- Work with celebrities like Justin Bieber, Kevin Hart, and Heidi Klum.

- Have a write-up in SLAM Magazine and other assorted newspapers.
- Write and have a book published about my life story to inspire kids to pursue their own dreams!
- Meet with some of the top business minds today to share my story.
- Give back to my hometown and neighboring communities in a powerful way.
- Build a platform and network, allowing me to create a youth program that will make a huge difference in the lives of kids around the world!
- Travel the world speaking, literally getting paid to run my mouth!

The crazy thing is, none of these things would have been possible if I hadn't embraced my fears. Fears of failing. Fears of not being able to pay my bills. Fears of what other people would think of me. Fears of passing up great corporate jobs with good pay and never getting those opportunities again. The easy choice would have been to get that safe job and work hard and live a good, safe life. There have certainly been bumps along the road, and points where I questioned if I was choosing the right path, but the struggle and challenges have made the rewards that much sweeter! I've chosen an unorthodox path for my life and continue to strive to do things that people tell me I cannot do. It's exciting to watch the progress I've made, and I've found that with every goal I've achieved, that which seemed so impossible and unlikely doesn't seem so far off.

I hope that is what you will take away from this book. Whatever it is you want in life, do it! Get rid of the excuses and limiting beliefs! Quit caring what other people think about you! (Why do we care about what other people think so much, anyways? Seriously!) I like to live by the motto, "What you think of me is none of my business!" Surround yourself with people who are successful and work your butt off to be the best you possibly can! I'm the last person who should be getting to do any of the things I just listed. I was an undersized kid from Alaska, for crying out loud! But I am doing those things because I made the decision that I was going to live this life with focus and passion, and I've put in the time and effort to start making my dreams happen.

"TWO ROADS DIVERGED IN A WOOD, AND I,

I TOOK THE ONE LESS TRAVELED BY,

AND THAT HAS MADE ALL THE DIFFERENCE."

—ROBERT FROST, AMERICAN POET

LIFE LESSON #15: ANYTHING IS POSSIBLE!

The choice is yours. What will you choose? I hope you will find, as I have, that the "giants" you fight against can be defeated, and that a whole new and exciting life can be yours when you tame your fears and work hard, pursuing your passion and dreams with complete determination and your whole heart!

See your dream before you. Believe in yourself and what you can accomplish. Chose to be all in. Do the work it takes; you can't hire out your push-ups.

And no matter what, when you meet the obstacles that *will* come your way, chose to stay all in, because that is the key to success. Anything is possible; you just have to make it happen.

PRE- & POST-SEASON TRAINING

MORE LIFE LESSONS FOR WINNERS

LIFE LESSON #16: EMBRACE YOUR UNIQUENESS!

WHAT IF YOU COULD TURN YOUR BIGGEST WEAKNESS INTO YOUR GREATEST STRENGTH? IN THIS VIDEO, I SHARE HOW THIS CONCEPT WAS A BIG BREAK THROUGH FOR ME.

I never really fit the mold for what a basketball player should look like. Although I worked extremely hard to become bigger, faster, and stronger, at the end of the day, I still looked younger and weaker than many other players. This caused me to think outside of the box, to embrace my uniqueness. How could being smaller be an asset for me instead of a liability?

For one thing, I was really fast, and I realized that being low to the ground could give me a big advantage when it came to dribbling. I was low enough to the ground that I could also disrupt most of my opponents when they were dribbling. I knew I would never be a shot blocker, but everyone had to bring the ball through my zone to get their shot off. I began to study the way people shot the basketball so I could swipe it away before they could shoot. I worked hard to develop my hand quickness by hitting the speed bag and doing other drills. By playing to my strengths, I was able to take a perceived weakness and turn it into a strength. I began to strip the ball away from opponents at a surprisingly high rate. Having good anticipation skills was also a key ingredient, but that's something you can develop as well.

Playing to my abilities was something that helped me get my start in acting as well. When I started, I was primarily going to auditions for basketball roles. Because it was usually assumed that they wanted your stereotypical looking basketball players (tall, ripped, black, etc.), I stood out. Many people would see that as a bad thing; instead, I embraced it and used it as a good thing. All the competition were big, strong, NBA-type athletes who could throw down monstrous dunks. But casting directors would need at least one white guy to hit that demographic. They also needed someone who could handle the ball well. That epiphany is what motivated me to practice and master all the tricks I can do now with a basketball. I could never jump as high, look as old,

> ## "I WAS MOTIVATED TO BE DIFFERENT IN PART BECAUSE I WAS DIFFERENT."
>
> —DONNA BRAZILE, AMERICAN AUTHOR AND POLITICAL ANALYST

or grow as tall as the competition. However, I could make sure no one could handle a ball as well as me, and that is what helped make me unique and allowed me to start booking jobs. If I hadn't embrace the way I looked and the skills I did have, it's very unlikely that I would have been very successful. Being smaller and looking much younger than my true age also began to help me get roles that played to my advantage. Embrace what makes you, you! So many people are afraid to be different. They are afraid what other people think and say about them. If you think and act like everyone else, then you will be like everyone else. Don't let your fear of being criticized or judged paralyze you to stay in the average zone. Do you really want to be like everyone else anyway? Embrace your individuality.

Embrace your uniqueness.

LIFE LESSON #17: DON'T BE AFRAID TO BE SELFISH!

LEARN WHY BEING 'SELFISH' CAN BE THE MOST UNSELFISH DECISION YOU EVER MAKE IN THIS VIDEO.

If you are going to achieve your goals, you have to learn to stop caring about what other people think of you. So many of people are consumed by worrying about what other people think of them. What will they say about this shirt? Do you think they are going to notice I have a pimple? This is so limiting! The sooner you can phase out this type of thinking the better.

In my life, I strive to be different. Why would you want to be like everyone else? A lot of the people I grew up around didn't like their jobs, were unhappy in their relationships, and generally felt unsatisfied with their lives. Misery loves company. Often, the people in these situations were only unhappy because the people around them were unhappy, and so they assumed that they should be unhappy, too. It's a shame that so many people feel they should imitate the thinking and actions of the people in their immediate environment.

Growing up, I used to go to my local rec center to work on my game. I didn't ever get to play with any current or ex-college basketball players, so I knew I had to do something different than all the other people there if I wanted to play college ball someday. I knew I had to improve all the little bits and pieces of my game so that I could limit my mistakes. Being as small as I was, this was as true as ever, but I knew what I had to do, and I executed it every time I went to the gym.

> "TO BE SUCCESSFUL, YOU HAVE TO BE SELFISH, OR ELSE YOU NEVER ACHIEVE. AND ONCE YOU GET TO YOUR HIGHEST LEVEL, THEN YOU HAVE TO BE UNSELFISH. STAY REACHABLE. STAY IN TOUCH. DON'T ISOLATE."
>
> —MICHAEL JORDAN, BASKETBALL PLAYER AND LEGEND

Most people don't realize how valuable gym time is. They will step onto the court with their shoes untied and throw up shots from half court, try to shoot it off the wall, and waste time they could have used to get better. My dad and I used to call these people "friendlies." They see you, and for whatever reason, they feel the need to shoot at the same basket as you. They get in your way and are an overall annoyance. I have no patience for these types of people. I would promptly tell them I was working out and either they needed to go to another basket or I would switch hoops myself. I take it personally when someone tries to prevent me from doing what I need to do to get to where I want to go. That's competitive fire, and I don't think you can be successful without it!

People would try to get me to run-full court games with them, but if there weren't players who would push me to get better, I wouldn't play. Sometime I would play in one game and when a new 'team,' full of guys who just wanted to mess around, would come on the court to play, and I would leave. People would get mad and yell at me, but I didn't care what they said or thought; I knew I had to do something different if I wanted a different result than everyone else. I wasn't there to play recreationally. I was an undersized point guard who had dreams of taking basketball as far as he could. Going against the grain and daring to be different helped me achieve what many people told me I would never be able to do. The funny thing is, the more I stood up for myself and told people what I was going to do, the easier it became, and the more people seemed to respect me for it. Don't be afraid to be your own person and do your own thing. There's plenty of time to help other people and be a giving person, but when it's work time, you can't hesitate to be "selfish" and expect people to respect what you are trying to do.

Don't be afraid to be selfish.

HERE'S A FUNNY VIDEO OF ME AS A YOUNGSTER AT CAMP. THIS IS WHERE THE CONCEPT OF "FRIENDLIES" WAS BORN!

LIFE LESSON #18: HAVE CHARACTER!

CHECK OUT THIS VIDEO MESSAGE AND SEE WHY HAVING HIGH MORAL CHARACTER CAN BE ONE OF YOUR BIGGEST ASSETS IN LIFE!

 omeone once described character to me this way: "Your character is who you are when no one else is watching." That is such a powerful statement. Growing up, I was told, "With every decision you make, you are deciding who you will be." When you start thinking in those kinds of terms, it can have a profound effect on how you view your choices. As I became more mature, this way of thinking started to resonate with me more and more, and changed me for the better. As I came into situations where I could do a minimal effort, not finish a job to the best of my ability, and get by without anyone knowing, I would hear the words of my parents in my head, and I instead chose to make the extra effort to do the right thing. Everything you do says something about you, good or bad. People remember you for your actions, and going the extra mile will earn you respect and open doors you never knew existed.

"HOLD YOURSELF RESPONSIBLE FOR A HIGHER STANDARD THAN ANYBODY EXPECTS OF YOU. NEVER EXCUSE YOURSELF."

—HENRY WARD BEECHER, AMERICAN CLERGYMAN AND SPEAKER

In Hollywood, the entertainment business is known for being very cutthroat. You hear about many people who forfeit their morals and step on people to make their way to the top. Friends betray friends in an effort to get ahead, and I've seen and experienced many of these things. I've also noticed that when you are genuine and put others first, you tend to attract similar people, and others will respect you more for staying true to your ethics and beliefs. A great example of living a life of character is Devon Franklin. I highly recommend his book, *Produced by Faith* which talks about pursuing your dreams without compromising your faith and morals. He shares his story of being a devoutly moral person in an industry that predominately shuns that sort of behavior. In the book, you'll learn how he overcame the odds and became one of the youngest and most impactful studio executives in Hollywood. He speaks on a regular basis, and if you have a chance, you should check him out. Devon shares how he took an unwavering stand for his beliefs and how, in the end, others respected him more for it. Stand for what you know is right, live with integrity, and look to serve others whenever possible.

Your reputation is your greatest asset. What do people say about you when you aren't around? Is it positive or negative? There's one thing you can be sure of: people are talking about you one way or another. Strive to be someone that others respect. The best way to do that is to live a life of high character. You can do so by making decisions that aren't just self-seeking but are in the best interest of others. Work hard, be a giver, and do the right thing. I believe each and every person has a conscience or moral compass inside of us, so listen to that little voice; it was put there for a reason.

An important quality that will improve your character is trust. Trust is the basis of every relationship and critical if you want to live a happy and successful life. You must trust others, and they must be able to trust you. Do people believe what you are saying? Being truthful and honest with others, as well as yourself, is a huge deal. It has been found that the most successful people are extremely honest about their own strengths, weaknesses, and abilities, and they own it. The good and the bad. Too many of us, myself included, are far too comfortable with lying to ourselves so we feel better about the things we aren't so proud of. We have to stop this behavior if we want to progress and be completely real with ourselves! By being a truthful person, you will find that others will respect you more and hold your opinion in higher regard. Mean what you say, and say what you mean. I challenge you to do so today.

Make good decisions.

LIFE LESSON #19: CREATE GOOD HABITS!

SEE WHY LITTLE HABITS CAN MAKE ALL THE DIFFERENCE IN YOUR LIFE IN THIS VIDEO.

 person's habits can make or break them. Our habits play a significant role in the direction of our lives. Positive habits result in positive outcomes, and negative habits result in negative outcomes. It's that simple. The key is to be honest with yourself and identify which habits you have that are good (washing your hands before you eat, brushing your teeth, consistently being on time, staying true to your word) and which habits aren't so good (wasting time, gossiping, not getting your work done, staying up too late,, eating junk food, smoking). Maybe you need a close friend to help you explore the habits in your life that you need to work on and also hold you accountable. Research shows us that the majority of our actions throughout the course of the day are habitual; we do them without even thinking. Become the master of your habits, and you can maximize your time management and productivity to the fullest!

Habits tend to work in the same way and follow certain patterns. First, there is a trigger, which can be a place, an emotion you are feeling at the time, or even certain people. Next, the habit or routine takes place. The final phase is the reward. If you can diagnose your habits, you can decide what the rewards will be. It simply comes down to this: what habits do you want to change?

> **"YOU CAN'T JUST QUIT A BAD HABIT; YOU HAVE TO REPLACE IT WITH A GOOD ONE."**
>
> —DR. PHIL, TV PERSONALITY AND HOST

With that being said, I'd like to share with you some insight from Stephen R. Covey's book, *The 7 Habits of Highly Effective People*, and give you some perspective from my experience with these principles.

BE PROACTIVE

Being proactive is all about taking action and ownership for your life, as well as creating opportunities and holding yourself accountable for the current state of your life. Everything around us is a direct result of our choices and our responses to the events that happen to us. It is easy to dwell on the things that aren't fair and are out of our control, but that is kind of like a rocking chair: it gives you something to do, but it doesn't get you anywhere. When you stop blaming outside factors and own your life completely, you will live an exponentially more happy, fruitful, and productive life. For me, being proactive has meant taking calculated leaps of faith, surrounding myself with the best people, owning my actions AND thoughts, and getting rid of excuses like "I'm too little," "Most people don't succeed in this industry," "I don't have enough experience to succeed at this," and "I'm too young to do that." There will never be a perfect time to do anything. You can always find an excuse, whether it's bad weather that time of year, the country is at war, the wrong president is in office, or there are health issues in the family. If you really want it, you have to put all that aside and just go for it! Make a habit of being proactive. Focus on the things you can control, and steer yourself in the direction that is going to lead you to success and happiness, whatever that means for you.

BEGIN WITH THE END IN MIND

It is important to have a long-term vision and goals for your life. Otherwise, it is easy to wander aimlessly and let the random external factors direct your path. One thing that can help you with this is finding your own personal mission statement. Nearly every company and business has one, and you should, too. What is your purpose in this life? What are you here for? We all know one of the greatest keys to personal happiness in life is giving. Giving gives us satisfaction and can lead to a much happier and more fulfilled life. Once you know what your personal mission statement is, you'll find that making decisions will be much easier. You can ask yourself, "Does this align with my mission?" If it does, great! If not, it's probably not the right choice for you. Find your true purpose, and your life will take on much more meaning as a result.

Visualizing where you want to be is key for getting there. It has been proven the body cannot tell the difference between reality and imagination when it comes to emotions. If you can use your imagination to create the feelings, smells, and emotions of your desired outcomes, your body truly believes that it's happening. This phenomenon is known by many as the law of the attraction. Whether you believe in a higher power such as God, Buddah, or just The Universe in general, there is power in our thoughts. We are what we think.

When you make a deliberate decision to focus on your long-term goals, that intention can help open doors and create opportunities for you that you may have never expected. Your subconscious mind starts figuring ways to get to where you want to be when you don't even realize it. You might be in the shower daydreaming and have a life-changing idea fly into your head out of nowhere. You can thank your subconscious mind and the law of attraction for that.

When I first made the decision to visualize and claim what I wanted my life to become, I started experiencing what seemed like a series of random coincidences. I started bumping into people who had the power to open doors that I never could. Random people were referred to me. Amazing ideas would come to me when I wasn't trying to come up with them. Opportunities I could only dream of came knocking at my door. After this started happening consistently, I realized I was experiencing the law of attraction firsthand, and it was powerful! By believing in myself and having positive thoughts while confidently telling others my goals, I've been able to radically change my life. Always keep your end goal in mind. Make it a habit. Try it for yourself, I am willing to bet your experience will be similar to mine!

PUT FIRST THINGS FIRST

Putting first things first is all about being okay not doing everything and living a more balanced life. Finding your priorities, sticking to them, and being okay with telling people no are invaluable habits to build. To be honest, this is something that I struggle with. I used to try to do everything all the time—respond to every email, take every call, meet every person that wanted to talk—and it exhausted me. One thing that helped me was making a daily to-do list the night before. That gave my subconscious mind the ability to figure out how I would get everything done all night, and it boosted my efficiency throughout the day. I would prioritize my daily agenda from the most important to the least important. I found that by putting the hardest task first and completing it in the morning, the rest of my day became a breeze. Instead of dreading those one or two things like I normally would, I would knock them out early, feel accomplished, and get much more done the rest of the day.

Then I learned about the 80/20 rule. The 80/20 rule states that 80 percent of your outcomes come from 20 percent of your inputs. For example, in business it is often proven that 20 percent of your clients produce 80 percent of your profits. The examples go on and on, but the key takeaway is that we need to focus more on the things that get us the most results! How much time do we waste on pointless emails, meetings, and small talk when you could be focusing on the 20 percent of things that make you the most happy and successful? If you are anything like me, you probably spend way too much time on the non-essential things. If you want to see big gains in your productivity and results, identify and dedicate more time to the 20 percent. I highly recommend you take a look at *The 4-Hour Work Week* by Tim Ferriss. He breaks down this principle to a science that will change the whole way you look at life. Get the results and life you desire, and start putting first things first!

THINK WIN-WIN

The attitude for thinking win-win comes from a spirit of seeking to serve others. When you look to put others first, you'll often find that others will want to help you in return. Many of us are programmed with the thinking that there isn't enough to go around, so we have to get "ours" if we are going to make it. Thinking win-win is the view that there is enough success to go around for everyone, and if we all work together, we can all achieve more. It takes honesty and courage to make this line of thinking a habit. You can't be afraid to ask for what you want, but always think in terms of how you and others can both benefit from different situations. Start trying to view life as more collaborative and less cut-throat, and you'll be thinking win-win!

SEEK FIRST TO UNDERSTAND, THEN TO BE UNDERSTOOD

Learning to be a great listener is one of the greatest skills you can ever learn. Being a strong communicator is key to success in life, but shutting up and being an active listener can be so hard to do—believe me, I know! By nature, most of us want to give our two cents, share our similar experience, and have others understand where we are coming from.

We have to stop doing this! I'll sometimes zone out or start planning what I am going to say while the other person is still speaking, holding out just long enough for the other person to take a breath before I jump in and say what I want to say. If you want to become a highly effective person, make the habit of simply closing your mouth and actually listening

> "I NEVER LEARNED ANYTHING NEW WHILE I WAS TALKING."
>
> —LARRY KING, AMERICAN TV AND RADIO HOST

to what people have to say. In my own life, I've actually been able to shut my mouth for a few minutes of time, believe it or not. As a result, I've seen first-hand that people trust me more and seek my advice, and I develop deeper and stronger relationships with people. I've also noticed that people want to volunteer a lot more information to me (not always a good thing) simply because they know I will listen. See growth in your relationships by lending your ear to listen to others first.

I know a crazy surfer who loves to use the catchphrase "Teamwork makes the dream work!" Or maybe you are familiar with the acronym for TEAM:

Together

Everyone

Achieves

More

That's what "synergy" is all about: the mindset that two heads are better than one. It is a very effective habit to always be looking for ways to collaborate with others and be open to new ideas. When you combine forces, your productivity and results increase exponentially. As my mother always used to say when it came time to do the dishes, "Many hands make light work."

One key to finding synergy with others is embracing your uniqueness and the uniqueness of others. It is easy to feel annoyed with or threatened by people who think differently or come from an entirely different background. It's much easier to surround ourselves with people who are always going to agree with us. But surrounding yourself with "yes men is dangerous and limiting. In order to grow, you need people in your life who are going to challenge, question, and push you. If no one around you has different views than your own, you are in a scary position. Find people who are different, and embrace them wholeheartedly. Look to synergize. Besides, the world would be a pretty boring place if everyone was just like you and me. Variety is the spice of life.

SHARPEN THE SAW

The hardest obstacle you will ever have to overcome is yourself! Learning how to maintain yourself so that you can operate at your highest level is critical for your success. It's important for you to learn how to protect your greatest asset which is, of course, you! We all know your body needs to be maintained with the proper nutrition, sleep and exercise, but keeping your mind clear and alert is equally important.

Keeping a sharp saw comes down to having balance in your life. There are four major areas highly effective people focus on. The first, possibly most critical, is your physical self. It can be nearly impossible to keep any type of order in your life if you don't have your health. As an athlete, my whole life I've learned the importance of staying fit and the many benefits that come along with it. Eating right, exercising, and getting enough sleep are the three main components when it comes to staying on top of health.

The second area to focus on is your social and emotional health. We were designed to build meaningful relationships with others, and when we don't have this type of outlet and make time to connect with others, we suffer.

The next area is your mental state. You can keep your mind sharp by continuing to learn and also by teaching others. Reading, writing, and solving crossword puzzles are all ways to stay mentally sharp and on top of your game. Don't let your brain go to mush; exercise it just like you would any other muscle!

Last, but not least, is keeping balance in your spiritual life. That might mean something different for everyone. For me it's praying, attending church, and going to yoga. For others, it may be hanging out in nature, creating art, or playing an instrument. Find what brings you peace, alleviates your stress, and allows you the most happiness. The key is to find balance in all things. Remember, it can be just as crippling to be a workaholic as it is to be out being social every night.

By keeping your saw (in this case, yourself) sharp, you will have the ability to operate at your highest level! Gain the edge and feel great, look great, and be happier by keeping proper balance in your life.

For a more in-depth look into these principles from Stephen R. Covey him-self, I encourage you to go check out his book, *The 7 Habits of Highly Effective People*. It's worth it!

Make good habits.

LIFE LESSON #20: BE LIKABLE!

BEING LIKABLE CAN TAKE YOU FURTHER IN LIFE. IF YOU DON'T BELIEVE ME, CHECK OUT THIS VIDEO!

 ave you ever met someone and immediately thought, *I like this person*. Of course you have. One quality I've observed from my most successful friends and acquaintances is that they all are extremely likable. You just like how you feel when you interact with them. I've found that people are naturally drawn to these people time and time again. As I began to notice this, I started paying closer attention to it. I wanted to know why everyone liked these people so much!

One of the people I first noticed this likability factor in was my close friend,

Taylor. Taylor stars on his own TV show on Nickelodeon, has had lead roles in several movies, and has an awesome new show coming out called *Star Wars Rebels*. Everywhere we go, people LOVE Taylor. I am no exception. I love that guy! He's always upbeat, encourages others, has a good heart, and no matter what's going on around him, he's always smiling! It's almost obnoxious! I mean, half the time I feel like he's playing some joke on me that I'm unaware of and he is getting a kick out of it. He is a witty kid and isn't afraid to give you a bad time, no matter how well he does or doesn't know you. Even though he has become like my little brother, I feel like I am constantly learning from his example, and I am so proud of him and the progress he continues to make in his career and growth as a young adult. His family has become like my own, and I am so appreciative that they accepted me and became my L.A. family. Taylor is a beast of an actor and will continue to do great things. I met Taylor when I was his basketball stunt performer in the movie *Thunderstuck*, starring Taylor and Kevin Durant.

> "THE MOST IMPORTANT SINGLE INGREDIENT IN THE FORMULA OF SUCCESS IS KNOWING HOW TO GET ALONG WITH PEOPLE."
>
> —THEODORE ROOSEVELT, 26TH US PRESIDENT

YOU CAN CHECK HIM (AND SOME OF MY MOVES) OUT IN THE MOVIE TRAILER HERE. FOLLOW TAYLOR ON TWITTER AND INSTAGRAM! @_TAYLOR_GRAY_

My best friend, and possibly the most likable man in America, is none other than Sinqua Walls. He has been on numerous TV shows such as *Friday Night Lights*, *The Secret Life of an American Teenager*, *Grey's Anatomy*, *Teen Wolf*, *Once Upon A Time*, and starred in the movie *Shark Night 3D*. He is one of the most humble guys I know and has the uncanny ability to be liked by everyone. He is a charismatic and handsome guy who carries himself with poise at all times. I've seen him say things to people that I'm pretty sure would get me slapped if I said them. Yet when he leaves the room, they say, "He's the real deal; that's a good guy right there!"

One of the things I've observed that I believe helps Sinqua be so likable is the fact that he smiles a lot, just like Taylor. He makes great eye contact, and he takes a very sincere interest in the lives of other people. He has an amazing sense of humor, isn't afraid to poke fun at himself, and continually talks about the other person more than himself. The conversation is always about the other person, and that, in turn, makes the people around him feel special. Sinqua is one of the most genuine people I have ever met, and I am proud to call him my best friend. Although we fight like brothers sometimes, I'll always have his back, and I am so excited for the things that lie ahead of him in his life because I know he is destined for greatness! If you are reading this, Sinqua, you have become my brother. I value our relationship, and I am so thankful for you and the positive influence you've had on my life. I love you, bro!

Another young, successful guy I have a lot of respect for is Mr. Hunger

> HERE'S A VIDEO OF SINQUA TAKING SOME TIME OUT OF HIS BUSY SCHEDULE AND SPEAKING TO KIDS AT A LOCAL SCHOOL ABOUT LEADERSHIP. YOU CAN FOLLOW SOME OF SINQUA'S CLEVER QUOTES AND PHRASES, OR AS WE CALL THEM, "QUAISMS," ON TWITTER @SINQUAWALLS

Games himself, Josh Hutcherson. Josh is an avid basketball fan and player, and we play in a few of the same leagues, so I've gotten to know him a little bit. He keeps an awesome circle of close friends, and his mom used to love heckling me from the sidelines when we played against each other! I immediately saw the same quality in Josh as I had in Taylor and Sinqua: likability! Every time we bump into each other, he goes out of his way to say "hi" to me first, ask me how I am doing, what I'm up to, or how my recent trip was. He really takes a sincere interest in my life, and I always walk away feeling like a million bucks. I don't even feel like he should be talking to me; he's so far out of my league, and yet he always continues to be so down to earth. I've never heard him talk about himself, even once; he doesn't take himself too seriously, and never once have I seen him act like he was better than anyone else. Here is a kid at the height of superstardom who could easily be cocky and think he's better than the people around him. Instead, he does just the opposite. He chooses to be humble. I love this quality about Josh, and I wish him nothing but success as his exceptional character and winner's approach to life continue to take him to the top! (You can follow Josh on Twitter at @jhutch1992)

It makes sense to me that these guys have done great in their acting careers because being likable is the name of the game in entertainment. You go into an audition and you are immediately judged by the director, and casting people. Do you have the right look, do you embody the essence of the character, do you have acting chops, do you seem like you'd be annoying to be on set with for six months, etc., etc.? But the underlying element that goes along with every audition is this: are you likable? The answer for these three guys is certainly YES, AND THEN SOME!

HERE I AM WITH MY FRIENDS TAYLOR, CHRIS WITH JOSH AT HIS ANNUAL CELEBRITY BASKETBALL GAME.

You don't have to be in the entertainment industry to benefit from being likable. It can help you in virtually every area of your life—school, work, re-lationships, you name it. Being an authentically likable good person will help you get so much further in life. To help you implement some strategies for becoming more likable, take a look at some notes I've compiled for you.

We all know people who just seem to have a likable personality and dispo-sition. Some people may come about this more naturally by their upbringing or personal choices, but everyone can implement actions into our behavior to be more liked by others. The following is a list I've taken from Dale Carnegie's *How to Win Friends and Influence People*, a book that has sold over 15 million copies. I would highly recommend reading this book, as it has played a pro-found part in my life when it comes to relating to other people. The benefits I have seen in my own life have been tremendous! I truly believe that being lik-able is one of the key components for being successful and happy in life! I hope the principles outlined below help you become more attractive to the people you encounter in your life.

SIX WAYS TO MAKE PEOPLE LIKE YOU

Become genuinely interested in other people.

For some people, this is harder to do than others. My dad was always a really big people person; he always asked others tons of questions about themselves and seemed sincerely interested. Was my dad using some universal law to try to be liked? No; he just liked people and took a keen interest in learning about them. That rubbed off on me, and I was much the same way. Growing up, there were plenty of times when I would meet someone (usually a female) and within half an hour they had told me their entire life story and intimate details they hadn't shared with anyone besides me and a few others. As this began to happen to me time after time, I learned that by taking a sincere interest in someone else and shutting your mouth to listen, you can really make a difference in someone else's life. All some people want is for someone to listen to them and actually care about what is happening in their life. By doing so, you earn their trust, and it doesn't even take that much effort. By having a good heart and just taking a little time to learn about someone new, you can make a huge impact on that person for the better. By doing this, you can make others feel so much better about themselves, and in turn they will want to do whatever they can to help their "new best friend." Start trying this in your own life and see how people react. We all want to talk about our lives, our problems, our accomplishments. But when we put that aside and put others needs first, we can learn so much. So stop talking about yourself and start focusing on listening to others; it's amazing what you'll learn!

Smile.

It's as simple as it sounds: smile. It's crazy how by merely smiling we can make others view us in a more positive light. When Taylor was a little kid, he started going out for commercials and started booking gigs at an amazing rate. In the time frame of two years, he was able to book over fifteen national commercials, and for those of you who aren't in the business, that is a lot! The average person is happy if they book two national spots a year. When I asked him what his secret for doing so well was, he told he only had one goal when he went into the auditions: smile the entire time he was in the room. Try it in your own life. When you walk by a stranger, coworker, or friend, shoot them a smile, and I can guarantee you will notice a change in the way people treat you and act towards you. People love to be around happy people because it makes them feel good about themselves.

Remember and use people's names.

A person's name is, to that person, the sweetest and most important sound in any language.

It's amazing how powerful remembering someone's name can be. I have to admit, I am horrible with names. One thing I have learned about myself over the years is that I am a very visual learner. If someone tells me their name, nine times out of ten, I am going to forget it. Then I started to notice how it made me feel when someone remembered my name. I felt important, and as a result, I was naturally drawn to like the people who remembered my name more. Once I realized this, I was much more motivated to learn a system that would make me better at remembering people's names. I started to ask people how they spelled their name, even if it was an easy name. That way, I could visually see the letters spelled out in my head, which in turn helped me become much better with name recall. Find what helps you with other people's names, and reap the rewards of being more likable to more people.

Be a good listener. Encourage others to talk about themselves.

How many times have you seen a person talk and talk and talk like they just love hearing their own voice and all you want them to do is shut up? Well, guess what? When you get long-winded, other people are thinking the same thing about you, and it's a huge turn off. Instead, allow others to ramble and carry the brunt of the conversation. Often, you'll find that you may not say a darn thing an entire conversation, but by the time you are done, the other person will say something like, "I really like you; I enjoy talking with you." I can't tell you how many times this has happened to me in both my business life and personal relationships. It has certainly been a challenge for me to shut my mouth, as I usually have a lot to say, and I generally tend think that what I have to say is more witty, interesting, and intelligent than my counterpart. We all think that way. Sometimes, I literally have the thought, "Just shut up, Jesse," and I force myself to listen, even when I don't want to, and especially when I don't agree with someone and I feel like they are wasting my time. Instead of trying to impress others by our fancy words and telling them how great we are, we need to take an interest in others and their lives. By doing so, you will strengthen the depth of your relationships, become more likable to a larger amount of people, and transform into an overall more giving and caring person. Listen to others, shut your mouth, and see the rewards grow in your life!

Talk in terms of the other person's interests.

Living in L.A., I feel like it is safe to say I spend a lot of time in one of the most self-centered, "look at me" places in the world. Everyone wants to show you how well they're doing, how nice their car is, how expensive their watch is, and how extravagant their house is. I think the vast majority of us can agree that this "look at me" attitude is a huge turnoff. Nobody wants to hear somebody talk about everything having to do with them all the time. If you want to be more likable, it is critical to talk in the terms of other people's interests. Find out what makes them tick. What are their hobbies? What is most important to them in life? How can you help improve the quality of their life by introducing them to a person or concept that could benefit them? Start talking in a way that is of interest to the people you are around, and you will see an increase in how many people want to be your friend and want to help you. It's funny, but it's true: when we look to help others, we are blessed in return. Find solutions to other people's problems, connect them with others that can be to their benefit, and do so expecting nothing in return.

Make the other person feel important—and do it sincerely.

People don't always remember what you said, but they will remember how you made them feel. Let me say it again. People don't always remember what you *said*, but they will remember how you made them *feel*. How do you make others feel on a daily basis? Do you drag them down and talk about your problems and your "woe is me" baloney? Are you only concerned about yourself and don't make an effort to see what other people are going through in their lives? Maybe you just avoid people all together? In my own experience, I can say with confidence that by doing all the things above (smiling, remembering people's names, being genuinely interested in them, etc.) you will naturally make people feel important and like they matter to you—which they should! If you live life only caring about your own selfish ambition, you have missed the boat entirely and will never truly be happy.

> "OUR ATTITUDE TOWARDS OTHERS DETERMINES THEIR ATTITUDE TOWARDS US."
>
> —EARL NIGHTINGALE, AMERICAN MOTIVATIONAL SPEAKER AND AUTHOR

Life is all about giving back and helping others. When you come to this realization and start living for something bigger than merely yourself, you will find you lead a much more meaningful existence.

Why is it important for people to like me? you may be asking yourself. *I have my friends, and I don't need any more.* Or *My business doesn't require me to build relationships for it to be successful.*

No matter what you do, where you live, or what your goals are, I can promise you this: your success depends on your ability to build strong relationships with the people around you. Whether it is in your career, education, family, or social interactions, we spend our entire lives building relationships. Don't you think it might be beneficial to build long-lasting, sincere relationships and be more liked by those you deal with on a daily basis? We often hear it said, "It's not what you know; it's WHO you know." But that isn't necessarily right. Just knowing someone isn't enough. By building strong relationships with deep and solid roots, you will find you have a lot more doors open for you leading towards the path of success and where you want to be.

Due to the environment and family I grew up with, I naturally was an over-the–top, upbeat personality who was always smiling and took a strong interest in the people around me. That was just how I was from a very young age. It was never anything phony, and as a result (and I like to think largely to my GREAT sense of humor and humility), I had a lot of friends, was popular in school, and found that people were for the most part always willing to go the extra mile for me when I was growing up. When I learned about these six principles, I became more conscious of them in my own life and started to apply them more. I almost find it funny that people don't just act this way normally. To this day, I continue to benefit personally and professionally from many meaningful relationships I've developed by putting these methods to practice.

By applying these principles to my life, I've seen such tremendous growth that it inspires me to share it with others.

You can be likable.

LIFE LESSON #21: BE YOUR BEST ALL THE TIME!

WATCH THIS VIDEO AND LEARN HOW TO OPERATE AT YOUR
HIGHEST LEVEL AT ALL TIMES.

ave you ever had a day where you went to bed and felt a sense of pride and accomplishment because you got so much done? Isn't that a great feeling? That's the feeling that successful people strive for every day in all areas of their life.

A lesson my dad imparted to me from day one was to always do everything to the best of my ability. I had lots of chores growing up, and many of them I wasn't too thrilled about. Those included chopping fire wood, picking rusty nails off the property (left over from a building which had burned down), trimming down salmonberry bushes, burning paper trash out on the beach, and many others which I found tedious. I remember one time, when I had kitchen duty, I cleaned up quickly and went along my way without giving it a second thought. My dad called me back, showing me the shoddy areas where there were still crumbs and debris, and a wet, wadded up wash cloth still laying in the sink. He told me,

"IF YOU ARE GOING TO DO SOMETHING, DO IT RIGHT, AND FINISH THE JOB. ALWAYS DO EVERYTHING TO THE BEST OF YOUR ABILITY. THAT'S WHAT PEOPLE WILL REMEMBER YOU FOR."

That talk made a lasting impression on me, and still pops up into my mind occasionally, especially when I know I'm being lazy and cutting corners. After that experience, I always tried to go the extra mile, whether it be getting a 4.0 GPA in school, giving it that little extra effort at practice, or leaving things better than I found them whenever I did any clean-up. You can tell a lot about someone by the kind of pride they take in what they do . . . especially when it involves something boring or tedious.

High performance is a concept that basically means to operate at your highest level in everything you do. You

"MY ATTITUDE IS THAT IF YOU PUSH ME TOWARDS SOMETHING THAT YOU THINK IS A WEAKNESS, THEN I WILL TURN THAT PERCEIVED WEAKNESS INTO A STRENGTH."

—MICHAEL JORDAN, BASKETBALL PLAYER AND LEGEND

have to be firing on all cylinders if you want to be able to accomplish all you possibly can in this life. This means being in peak physical shape. Do you consistently get eight hours of sleep? Are you drinking enough water? Are you exercising every day? Are you putting the right foods in your body? Do you have balance in your life between work, family, and play? Are you maximizing your time and abilities to complete as much as you need to everyday by prioritizing your schedule the night before? All of these factors are important if you are serious about operating at your highest potential.

To learn more about how you can be your best self every day, I encourage you to attend Brendon Buchards "High Performance Training." He is the best in the business and can increase the results in your life dramatically.

Live a high performance life.

HERE'S A SHORT VIDEO BY BRENDON ON HIGH PERFORMANCE.

"THE WILL TO SUCCEED IS IMPORTANT, BUT WHAT'S MORE IMPORTANT IS THE WILL TO PREPARE."

—BOBBY KNIGHT, FORMER NCAA BASKETBALL COACH

LIFE LESSON #22: FORGIVE!

STOP HOLDING ONTO BITTERNESS AND LEARN TO FORGIVE OTHERS. IT WILL TRANSFORM YOUR LIFE FOR THE BETTER! LEARN WHY IN THIS VIDEO.

orgiveness is such a powerful thing, and granting it can be so hard to do at times. It has changed my life for the better several times. Being an intensely competitive person, it can be hard to give someone a free pass when they have wronged me. I talked about a few of the terrible coaches and other people I had to deal with during my college years that ruined my last years of organized basketball. It's tough just moving on and not wanting to even the score or see them fail at what they are doing when karma slaps them in the face. It's human nature to want this, but it's the wrong attitude, and feeling that way actually hurts you in the end. After praying, reading the Bible, and speaking with people I respected, it became clear that I was only hurting myself by holding onto these people. I was consumed with wanting to see them be wronged in a similar fashion that they wronged me, and it gave them power over me as I wasted time thinking and fantasizing about different scenarios I would love to see happen.

I've had people wrong me in every way you could imagine. I've had the climax of my basketball career ruined by vindictive coaches; I've been treated with less respect than anyone should ever be while being ripped off thousands of dollars by greedy fishing boat captains; I've had roommates who told all our friends lies about me; I've had jealous friends try to ruin my character with people in the business I am in; I've had people laugh at me and tell me I was too small and wasn't good enough to play basketball in college; I've been told I would never be in a commercial, and I was an idiot for even thinking I could be. I didn't deserve these things, but we live in an imperfect world. I spent time being bitter and working harder to prove these people wrong. The best way to get back at someone is forgiving them and going on to live a great life!

> **"WE THINK THAT FORGIVENESS IS WEAKNESS, BUT IT'S ABSOLUTELY NOT; IT TAKES A VERY STRONG PERSON TO FORGIVE."**
>
> —T.D. JAKES, AUTHOR AND PASTOR

When I decided to forgive all these people, a huge weight was lifted off my shoulders. I could physically feel it. My mind was clear to focus on the things that I could do to move on with my life and be successful. I saw a direct correlation between my forgiveness and positive things happening in my life. The funny part is, all the people who hurt me in the past probably, at one point or another, while sitting at home watching TV, have seen me run across their TV screen! God works in mysterious ways, and when I forgave these people and left revenge to God, the result was much better than anything I may have fantasized about doing. Take the high road, and free yourself of wasted energy. Allow your mind to be cleared, and let God bless you with the plans He has for your life. Once you feel the power of forgiveness in your life, you'll be happy you did. Don't allow someone who isn't worth your time to have power over you!

Choose to forgive.

HERE IS AN AWESOME VIDEO BY LEGENDARY MOTIVATIONAL SPEAKER ZIG ZIGLAR. HE'S OLD SCHOOL, BUT HE'S AN AMAZINGLY WISE MAN WHO HAS HAD A TREMENDOUS IMPACT ON ME OVER THE YEARS.

"BEAR WITH EACH OTHER AND FORGIVE WHATEVER GRIEVANCES YOU MAY HAVE AGAINST ONE ANOTHER. FORGIVE AS THE LORD FORGAVE YOU."

—COLOSSIANS 3:13

LIFE LESSON #23: BE HUMBLE! DON'T BE THE LOUDEST PERSON IN THE GYM!

LEARN WHY BEING HUMBLE IS CRITICAL TO YOUR SUCCESS IN THIS VIDEO.

Many people love to talk about themselves! One thing that I've learned from living a few years in L.A., is that many, many, MANY people are full of it. At first, I didn't get this. Why would people lie about what they do and about their lives? It made no sense. I thought I was just randomly meeting very interesting people who were up-and-coming rap artists, music producers, actors, and part-time astronauts! As I went around the "block" a little more, I got wiser . . . and I began to realize that many of these folks were just blowing smoke. In nearly every case, the ones who were lying to me were not actually successful or doing anything truly exciting. They basically had a fan club of one.

It still baffles me why some people need to lie about what they are up to. I don't care if you are a janitor on "Dancing with the Stars"; it has no effect on me and my life. If anything, once I find out you are fabricating an imaginary life, then I don't really want to associate with you at all. I don't like being lied to, plain and simple.

Where I live in Hollywood, there are a lot of big talkers. Every time I see them, they're sitting around the pool in a group—usually in the middle of the day—just talking away with each other. Often, they try to suck me into their conversations about this and that, and go on and on about all the things they are going to do. It's a huge waste of time, and I have learned how to deal with them cordially and swiftly. If I can, I try to avoid them completely. When that's not an option, I'm pretty good at faking a phone call so I can keep moving. I'm a pretty outgoing and friendly guy by nature, so it has taken me awhile to be able to blow people off and not feel bad about it. I had to come to the realization that these people wanted to talk about success, but I wanted to get out and work for it. Michael Jordan sums it up beautifully:

"SOME PEOPLE WANT IT TO HAPPEN, SOME WISH IT WOULD HAPPEN, OTHERS MAKE IT HAPPEN."

When you strive to be someone who makes it happen, you can only do that by taking action. If you walk the walk, you don't have to talk the talk. In fact, you don't have to talk at all.

It's the same thing when you walk into the gym at a random place to hoop.

There is always that one guy who feels the need to talk the whole time. He wants everyone to be aware whenever he makes a shot or a good pass, and he is always his biggest fan! If he makes a mistake, he always has an excuse, and he just has to tell you about it. I'm sure you know the type. This guy is just annoying to be around. My point is this: if you are really a ball player, your game will speak for itself. You don't have to wear seventeen sweatbands all over your body and scream or yell to act the part of a stud. That doesn't fool anyone. Be yourself, and in all aspects of your life, let your actions, and the people around you, do the talking about you! Everyone will respect and like you more for it. Talk is cheap.

As I became more aware that people were telling me less than the full truth, I started to observe others more closely. I saw that my successful friends (who were already on TV and in movies) downplayed their careers and accomplishments. Some simply refused to bring them up at all. In one instance, I knew my friend had just read for Michael Bay and Tyler Perry for two different movies. In my mind, this was kind of a big deal. I wasn't even the person who was up for the roles, and I was excited about it! We got into a conversation with another friend of ours, a friend who can be something of an exaggerator. He was telling us one thing after another and going on and on and on about all that was happening in his career. Eventually, he finished and began to show an interest in what was going on with us. I looked over at my friend, expecting him to share some of his cool news. To my surprise, he didn't! Not one word. I was shocked. In fact, I found out later he had even bigger things going on behind the scenes that he hadn't even told me about!

After that incident, I started noticing that other successful people in the

> **"THERE ARE LOTS OF PEOPLE WHO MISTAKE THEIR IMAGINATION FOR THEIR MEMORY."**
>
> —JOSH BILLINGS, WRITER AND HUMORIST

entertainment industry behaved the same way. In many cases, they would downplay what they did or choose not to talk about themselves altogether.

My point is this: If you're really doing interesting and amazing things, you won't have to say anything about it. Plus, the sense of personal accomplishment you gain with every success is far more satisfying than any kind of recognition. But if you're dying for recognition, just trust me: people will find out eventually, one way or another, and once they do, they will be far more impressed that they didn't learn it through your bragging. Be humble. Don't be that abrasive person who is all swept up with themselves. The next thing you know, others will respect you more and have good things to say about you.

Whatever you do, don't be the loudest guy in the gym. Even better, don't even be friends with the loudest guy in the gym. Better still: Try to find a different gym!

Be humble.

"I HAVE NEVER BEEN HURT BY WHAT I HAVE NOT SAID."

—CALVIN COOLIDGE

LIFE LESSON #24: LEARN FROM OTHERS!

THIS VIDEO AND CHAPTER CAN HELP ACCELERATE YOUR LIFE AND SAVE YOU YEARS OF WASTED TIME, FRUSTRATION, AND MONEY.

 ven a fool, when he holdeth his peace, is counted wise" (Proverbs 17:28). Or, as Abraham Lincoln put it:

"BETTER TO REMAIN SILENT AND BE THOUGHT A FOOL THAN TO SPEAK AND REMOVE ALL DOUBT."

WHEN TO BE SILENT:

I love the above quote from Proverbs because it's so true! When we can manage to keep our mouths shut, not only will we be able to learn from others; they may even think we are wise. How many times have you been in a conversation when the least knowledgeable person sees themselves as the expert and does most of the talking? I see it all the time! As they try to impress people with their baloney, secretly everyone is rolling their eyes at each other wishing the guy would just STOP already.

Conversely, if you are quietly listening and occasionally chime in with something you are well versed in, others will tend to pay a little more attention to your input and have a higher level of respect for your words. The less you speak, the more others will value your input. I call this "Calculated Silence." Calculated Silence can give the appearance of authority and can make you a stronger leader in the eyes of others. You need to speak seldom, but when you do, make it something important, and then give others a moment to process your words before speaking again.

I have a friend who did some motivational speaking on a US tour with with a very famous comedian whose name I can't say. But you definitely know who this guys is. They struck up conversation after one of the shows, and the world renown comic told my friend, "You're a good speaker, but you need to learn to listen to your audience. Their laughter, or their silence, is their response to you. You need to take time to pause and listen, and you'll connect better with your audience."

What a great piece of advice from one of the most successful "funny guys" in the world. Practice talking less and listening more to the people you interact with at work, in your school, and even in your family. There is nothing wrong with silence. In fact, silence can create very powerful moments for your words to sink in. Try it, and see how that simple practice can change things up for you . . . for the better.

WHEN TO LISTEN MORE, AND WHEN TO ASK QUESTIONS:

I had a baseball coach in Little League who was a nice guy, but he was more of a dad who kindly volunteered his time than an actual coach. He had never played baseball growing up (which was obvious and a bit comical when he tried to pitch batting practice or hit fly balls to the outfielders), but you could tell he had read a couple of "How To Coach Baseball For Kids in 90 Days" books. He had read just enough to give himself a false sense of security coaching our team. Instead of seeking advice from seasoned coaches and players, he took the "I am the most knowledgeable coach in the history of the sport of baseball" approach. I was an avid Little Leaguer, and I remember asking another team's coach (one who had played baseball his whole life and really knew the game) what he thought about my coach and the way he ran our team. I was ten years old, but I'll never forget what he said. He told me,

"NO MATTER HOW LONG I'VE BEEN PLAYING OR COACHING, THERE IS ALWAYS SO MUCH MORE I CAN LEARN ABOUT THE GAME! YOU HAVE TO BE LIKE A SPONGE AND ABSORB AS MUCH INFORMATION AND KNOWLEDGE AS YOU CAN ABOUT BASEBALL BECAUSE THE LEARNING NEVER STOPS. NOBODY HAS IT ALL FIGURED OUT, NO MATTER WHAT LEVEL THEY ARE AT . . . EVEN A "LIMITED" COACH MIGHT HAVE ONE PEARL OF WISDOM THAT CAN TAKE YOUR GAME TO THE NEXT LEVEL AND MAKE YOU A BETTER PLAYER."

Wow! What a huge lesson this was for me.

I continue to be amazed at how sports teach us so much about life. Whether or not I was ever going to make it to the major leagues or get a baseball scholarship to college, there were more important lessons in the big scheme of things. Learning to be open minded and still learn from people who appear "less than" capable, or who are offensive in nature and maybe rub me the wrong way with their abrasiveness, has been a monumental life lesson that has served me well over time. The learning never stops! If you reach a point in your life where you stop seeking to learn from others, or you hit a point where you think you have it all figured out . . . you'd better check yourself, because you might just be lost in La-La Land.

There are hidden gems of wisdom all around you. Seriously, be on the lookout for them! They can come from a teacher, a parent, your crazy Aunt Carly, your boss, or the janitor at your school. I can promise you that some of the people around you—even the ones you'd least expect—can have some monumental ideas that can radically change your health, family, finances, etc., for the better. Be willing to take the time to actively listen and reap some surprising benefits!

I love to talk. Those who know me well know I can be real chatterbox. I love to entertain my good friends with humor and various antics, and I also can talk smack (good-naturedly, of course) with the best of them. Learning to shut my big mouth and listen hasn't come easily to me, but with hard work and self-reminders, I am learning to get better at it. The benefits I've experienced from simply listening, as well as taking a genuine interest in the speaker, have been incredible to me! It is one of the most powerful gifts you can give to another human being: the courtesy and respect of just listening to them. I have likewise found that when I really listen to someone, their response is incredible. They seem to listen harder, show more interest and respect, and have a desire to help me if they are in a position to do so.

We all enjoy having others take an interest in us. If we are just able to shut our trap long enough to listen to others, we find that the returns are deeper and more sincere than we would otherwise experience. So many doors have opened for me since I've started letting other people talk more! I know it can be challenging to listen to others when you have something good you want to share, or you are biting back a rebuttal to put them in their place, but talking less and listening more is definitely something you need to try. See the results for yourself. I've been able to build stronger relationships in business, with friends, and with "romantic" partners tenfold.

Of course, there are some important times to speak. In the context of your everyday life, there are many benefits to asking questions. You both give and get people's attention. You have a type of control in the situation. You are able to get others talking and opening up, allowing you to build a stronger relation-ship. It shows that you care and is a basic way to respectfully show interest in the person and what they do. Though you receive many benefits when you ask questions, it's not about manipulating anyone to get something from them; it's about learning to present yourself in a genuine and authentic way. It's about learning how to take yourself out of the center of every circle and become teachable. It's humbling, and it builds character, which is essential to becoming successful in every aspect of your life.

WHY IT'S IMPORTANT TO LEARN HOW TO ASK GOOD QUESTIONS:

This concept is even more important as you pursue your dreams and build your career. Knowing how to ask good questions is a skill you must learn. "Closed mouths don't get fed," but they also don't get fed by asking pointless questions. You can save yourself a boatload of wasted time by asking smart questions to the right people.

We talked earlier in this book about surrounding yourself with successful people and being a sponge. Hopefully you've started to do that, so now it's time to start asking questions and start learning! I hate wasting time and learning the hard way by trial and error. I've saved myself valuable time, and made incredible strides in my career, by asking smart questions to the right people. Remember, even the most successful people enjoy giving advice and discussing their lives; if you ask questions that show you are not just randomly looking for insignificant information, they'll answer you. When you ask deeper questions, the response is generally always positive. Seek knowledge by first asking questions that allow others to talk about themselves in a positive light. Then, take a sincere personal interest in what they have to say. Let the conversation be about them, not you. Consider these examples:

"What do YOU think of this or that?"

"How did YOU approach this problem or situation?"

Now comes the important part: LISTEN! Listen actively and genuinely care about what they have to say. After some of this, you'll find people saying things like, "Wow, I've been talking the whole time! What about you? What do you have going on these days?" Now that you have them warmed up and they can see that you care, you can ask your questions. Keep them concise and direct. Once again, here comes the key: LISTEN! Stop thinking about what you are going to say next; bite your tongue and hear.

Ask questions that others don't, and show the person that you have some

> ## "WISDOM IS THE REWARD YOU GET FOR A LIFETIME OF LISTENING WHEN YOU'D HAVE PREFERRED TO TALK."
>
> —DOUG LARSON, AMERICAN COLUMNIST AND EDITOR

understanding of the topic and that are interested in them and what they are saying. When they can see you have done some homework on the subject (and perhaps on them), it is obvious that what they think and feel is important to you. So don't be afraid to ask, ask, ask . . . but make sure you ask good and smart questions.

Learn from others.

LIFE LESSON #25: DON'T WASTE TIME ON SOCIAL MEDIA!

COULD YOU BENEFIT FROM HAVING MORE FREE TIME, CLARITY, AND FOCUS IN YOUR LIFE? LEARN HOW TO GET THE UPPER-HAND ON THE COMPETITION AND WATCH THIS VIDEO.

ocial media has really changed the everyday lives of today's generation. It's crazy how powerful technology can be. Kids today are being "cyber-bullied," and many feel the need to exercise their right to free speech in an absurd way. Everybody is their own rockstar on Facebook, Twitter, Instagram, and other social media sites. Many people (especially younger ones) fail to realize that whatever you put up on the internet is out there *forever*. Proceed with a lot more caution if you want to avoid serious problems in the future. There's a whole generation coming up who are in for a rude awakening when it comes time to get a job. Companies can and will do background investigating. But what's even scarier is the amount of time people waste on social media! From posting pictures and updates to just sitting there non-stop all day reading about what everyone else is doing (or pretending to) is such an incredible waste of time! Go live your life! There is nothing to gain from knowing every status update that happens on your timeline. It's shocking to think how much a person could actually accomplish if they channeled that wasted time toward a good purpose. They could absolutely improve the quality of their life and others around them. In the time we waste on social media, we could alternatively (to name just a few things):

- learn another language,
- find a new stream of income that would allow us more freedom,
- volunteer to help for a cause we are passionate about,
- improve our personal fitness and live a healthier life, or
- spend more time strengthening our relationships.

What is your social media holding you back from? Time management is critical if you want to accomplish goals and reach your dreams. You can spend time enjoying social media, but be careful not to let it be your master. I allow myself ten minutes in the afternoon and ten minutes at night to respond to people each day. Staying with this commitment has improved my productivity tenfold! I used to waste more time involved with socializing electronically than I care to admit. It was a time–robber—and still can be. Make a smart commitment to yourself in this area. Operate at your highest productivity level, and limit your social media addiction as much as possible!

Don't waste your time.

LIFE LESSON #26: LET HATERS MOTIVATE YOU!

WHAT OTHER PEOPLE THINK ABOUT YOU IS NONE OF YOUR BUSINESS. IF YOU WANT TO LIVE A HAPPIER LIFE WATCH THIS VIDEO.

 o matter what you do, there will always be those around who belittle you, try to discourage you, or enjoy any failure you might experience. Learn sooner rather than later in your life not to listen to the negative words of naysayers. Unless someone who cares about your well-being is giving you constructive advice to further you toward your dreams and character, tune them out. We give others power over us when we care too much what they think about us. We all desire to be liked by others, but when you jeopardize your own happiness by allowing another person's perceptions to influence how you feel about yourself, then it becomes a problem.

This quote from Dave Ramsey sums it up pretty well:

"WE BUY THINGS WE DON'T NEED, WITH MONEY WE DON'T HAVE, TO IMPRESS PEOPLE WE DON'T LIKE."

Funny, but it's so true, isn't it? Why would we care? What another person thinks of me has no relevance to my life, so why waste my energy on it? Just do what makes you happy. Don't sweat the small stuff; life is too short.

Those who don't waste time worrying about what other people think tend to be a lot happier, more successful, and more productive. Life really is too short to waste time worrying about others opinions. Ironically, when we think everyone is talking and thinking about us . . . they aren't; they are too busy worrying about what other people think of them!

I heard a funny idea once called the 18/40/60 rule. It goes like this:

"At 18 years old, I worried about what everyone thought of me. At 40 years old, I didn't care what anyone thought of me. Now, at 60, I've finally realized that nobody has been thinking about me anyway!" What a bunch of narcissists we are. Too many of us, myself included, are far too caught up with our image; it's because we are insecure and want to be liked and respected. The best thing each one of us can do is be confident in ourselves. Own every part of yourself, flaws and all. If you are short and pale like me,

> ## "I DON'T KNOW THE KEY TO SUCCESS, BUT THE KEY TO FAILURE IS TO TRY TO PLEASE EVERYBODY."
>
> —WELL KNOWN QUOTE

rock it with pride! Who cares? At the end of the day, the only opinion that matters about yourself is your own. What other people think about you is none of your business.

I really respect those who aren't afraid to chase their dreams, say what they believe, and not care about negative opinions from those who don't really care about them. I want to be more like that! I still care a lot what other people think. I hate to let people down, it bothers me when people don't like me, and I want people to know I sincerely mean things when I say them. Although there is nothing wrong with wanting to be liked, we can't let our worries get in the way of our goals.

A couple men who really embody this principle and don't live their lives trying to obtain approval from the masses are Ted Nugent and Donald Trump. Whether or not you like their politics or personalities, neither one of these men is afraid to "tell it like it is"—at least how they see it. They don't normally apologize if their viewpoint offends people (which it usually does), nor do they pander to what is "politically correct," even though it would make them far more popular with the masses. In spite of this (or maybe because of it), they are successful on a massive scale. You don't become a rich businessman with major influence or a famous rock star without offending a few people along the way. But

> **"A SUCCESSFUL MAN IS ONE WHO CAN LAY A FIRM FOUNDATION WITH THE BRICKS OTHERS HAVE THROWN AT HIM."**
>
> —DAVID BRINKLEY, AMERICAN NEWSCASTER

I respect the way they stand for what they believe in and don't back down from it. I also think they are brilliant for staying relevant in the media by purposely saying controversial things that garner attention, but that's a conversation for another time and place. Follow "Uncle Ted" on Twitter at @TedNugent and keep tabs on his latest TV shows, tours, and other shenanigans that are shaking up America at www.TedNugent.com.

There's a saying that goes, "Let your haters be your motivators." It's a corny line, but there is some truth to it. One of the biggest driving forces for me in pursuing my different goals has been to prove the negative people around me wrong. When people doubted or told I wouldn't be able to do something, it instantly lit a fire under me!

When people told me I wasn't big enough to play basketball (or that I was too white), I immediately kicked it into overdrive. I would visualize myself succeeding and making the big plays while I practiced, and I would imagine the looks on their faces when I proved them wrong! When I was working on a fishing boat in Alaska and made the decision that I was going to move to Hollywood, I was met with aggressive negativity and doubt. The people I was working with all seemed to give the same sarcastic response: "Oh, you are going to move to Hollywood and be an actor . . . real original . . . I'm sure that will work out."

Once, I accidently left a list of some of my short- and long-term goals out on the galley table. One of the goals I had on there was to be in a national commercial with my friend Airdogg. I remember the captain's son seeing that and having lots to say about it, and none of it was meant to build me up. That only made me more determined to make it happen. The beauty is, I actually accomplished that goal . . . many times over, in fact. I know that my "friendly critic" has probably seen me and Airdogg (and Charles Barkley, Rajon Rondo, Dennis Rodman, Blake Griffin, etc.) running across his TV screen while he was sitting on the couch eating junk food! I've never had to say anything about my successes to my "haters" . . . my work has done the talking for me. An extremely wise person (my mother) once said, "The best revenge is forgiving and moving on to live an amazing life."

At the end of the day, though, you don't want your sole motivation to be proving people wrong. You need to be motivated by your own passion. If proving people wrong was my only goal, I never would have lasted. I wouldn't have played college ball. I wouldn't have been in commercials, movies, or nationally televised streetball games . . . with celebrities and famous professional athletes. Most importantly to me, I wouldn't have been able to create my Fab4 Takeover program and create a platform to help millions of kids around the world. I also know that just trying to prove my haters wrong wouldn't have been enough motivation to get me through the tiresome and lengthy process of writing and publishing a book. Channeling doubt and negativity and turning it into part of my motivation definitely helped stoke my ambitious fire, but more importantly, I was fueled by my love of the game of basketball and the desire to be the best I could be. I've also been driven by my passion to help kids, to make a difference, and succeed in an industry that is considered one of toughest in the world. Let your "haters" give you the edge you need to push even harder than you already are, but don't let them become your focus.

Let your haters be your motivators.

LIFE LESSON #27: BE A GIVER! SERVE OTHERS!

LEARN THE POWER OF GIVING IN THIS CHAPTER'S VIDEO MESSAGE.

A driving force behind my passion to excel and be successful is my desire to be able to help people on a large scale. Sometimes I have to remind myself not to get lost in my long-term vision, and to continue to help people along the way in my journey. It's funny, though, because I've found that the more I give selflessly, the more I seem to receive in return.

The Bible tells us that it's better to give than to receive, and it's true—even though it might not make sense at first. I mean, most people would rather be given a jet ski than spend a day working in the soup kitchen, right? But by giving, we balance our more selfish interests and find that we like ourselves a bit better for not being so self-centered. My parents used to tell me to "always leave things better than you found them," and I've discovered that this principle doesn't just apply to cleaning up the messes we make. Every time we interact with another person, we should do what we can to leave them feeling better than they did before. If we truly serve someone, we can change their life for the better. Applying this principle to people and situations makes me a better person, a better employee, a better friend, and a better motivator for others as I lead by example. It also contributes to my own sense of self-worth.

> "AS EACH HAS RECEIVED A GIFT, USE IT TO SERVE ONE ANOTHER, AS GOOD STEWARDS OF GOD'S VARIED GRACE . . ."
>
> —1 PETER 4:10 (ESV)

By giving, we also enable what I like to call intelligent self-interest. Society has drilled into our heads that self-interest is a bad thing, but from my perspective, it's not. At the end of the day, the more successful a person is, the bigger platform they have to help others. When you develop real relationships and give of your time, money, or expertise, the giving comes back around to you—often from places you never even dreamed were possibilities. If your heart is in the right place and your motives are pure, giving starts the receiving process.

All of us have been blessed with different talents, abilities, and drives. When I have used mine to help and encourage others, I have had some of the most fulfilling experiences of my life. I'm not suggesting that we serve other people because it makes us feel good, but it is the greatest bonus we get back!

There are so many ways to help other people, and it can be as simple as saying some words of encouragement. I learned how to encourage others from playing baseball and other sports. I loved Little League baseball as a kid, and my dad understood the big picture of the game and taught me how to play it the right way. I embodied everything he taught me. I sprinted on and off the field between every inning; it didn't matter if I struck out or made an error. I was a fireball of hustle and, most importantly, a steady stream of positive chatter towards my teammate.

Looking back, I can almost say it was too much; I never shut up! I think I drove a lot of people crazy, especially the opposing team. But my dad taught me that the people around me needed encouragement. That lesson has stuck with me to this day, and it has become one of my best qualities. Especially in such a competitive business and atmosphere, sincere encouragement is sometimes the best gift I can give the people I come in contact with. As you interact with others in school, on sports teams, at work, and in every situation in life, take the time to let them know you support and believe in them. You'll be amazed at the relationships you can build and the changes you can influence in the people, and the world, around you. It's an easy way to make a difference, and it leaves a lasting impression on others.

Another form of giving I strongly believe in is tithing and charitable donations. No matter your religious beliefs, it is important to donate a generous percentage of your income to those in need.

I try to give 10 percent of my income. In my experience, it seems like that 10% tends to be just the amount that takes me from a level of monetary security to a point of stress. I manage my money very tightly, and as a struggling actor, there have been many times when I didn't know where the money would come from to pay my bills if I donated that percentage. In the end, though, I believe God has blessed me time and time again, beyond whatever I gave in tithing during those times when money was tight. It's crazy how far a little faith can go. I have found that when I give to others, it comes back around tenfold. I don't give with the intention of getting something back in return, but more often than not, that's exactly what happens.

For example, a few months after I moved to L.A., I was nearly broke, but it was really on my heart to tithe. I ended up giving a large chunk of money to a friend for a missionary trip, but it left me unable to pay rent. I didn't know what I was going to do or where the rent money would come from. A few days later, I booked a huge commercial that I didn't think I had a shot at. I believe that God's hand was in that situation and that my obedience to Him in tithing was the reason I landed what turned out to be an awesome commercial. No matter what you believe, always be grateful for what you have and willing to share your success. No amount of monetary success will make you a successful person until you have the faith to give—not expecting anything in return. I can promise you that your generosity will make your life more full and happy and will make the world a better place.

Be a giver, and serve others.

LIFE LESSON #28: HAVE A GOOD ATTITUDE!

YOU CAN BE A WINNER OR A LOSER IN LIFE, THE CHOICE IS UP TO YOU. SEE WHY YOUR ATTITUDE WILL DETERMINE YOUR FUTURE IN THIS VIDEO.

I once heard a story about a guy who kept having unfortunate things happen to him. First his car broke down, and while his wife fumed and used every colorful word in the dictionary, he remained calm and poised as if nothing had happened. This seemed to upset his wife even more, and she laid into him: "Don't you even care that our car broke down again and now we have to pay a lot of money to have it fixed?"

He looked at her sincerely and replied, "The car broke down; I can get mad and frustrated and be upset, or I can stay upbeat and not let it ruin my day. Either way, the car will be broken down. I choose to be happy."

When they finally got home, he was at dinner with his family, and a baseball came smashing through the window and into the kitchen. Again, the wife came unglued while her husband remained unmoved, cleaned up the mess, and talked to the boys who lived next door and gave them their baseball back. As they sat back down to eat, the wife grilled him, saying that he better have given those boys a piece of his mind and how much of an inconvenience it would be to replace the window. His lack of anger once again upset her, and she blurted out, "Don't you even care that this happened?"

He casually told her, "The window is broken. I can get jump up and down and yell at the neighbors until I lose my voice, or I can clean up the mess and enjoy my dinner. Either way, the window will still be broken. I choose to be happy and enjoy my dinner and evening with you."

I think you get the idea. Attitude is a choice! It isn't always an easy choice, but with practice and positive self-talk, you can become the master of your own attitude. Every day, things are going to happen to us that are out of our control, but there is always one thing we can control: how we choose to react and let it affect us. If you learn to be in total control of your attitude, keep your temper in check, and keep the big picture in mind, your life will be so much better. People will be drawn to you, and you will have a huge advantage over others who don't have this principle figured out. It's great practice for becoming mentally tough, which will help you in so many different areas of your life. All in all, choosing to make the best of every situation is a key to being successful.

I recently was at a stop light, and the car in front of me decided to throw it in reverse and smash into the front of my car. Obviously this did not make me happy, but this offered me a great opportunity to work on choosing to have a positive attitude. This is something I've worked on many times before, often failing more than I would like to admit. The driver ahead of me walked back to me and timidly asked if I was okay. Long story short, I treated this stranger as if he were my long lost best friend, and he must have thanked me about ten times for being "so cool." Later that night, I got a text from him. He said he believes that everything happens for a reason, and he wanted to know what I did for a living. I told him and discovered that he is a producer, and one day he may want to pull me in on one of his projects. Who would have thought that simply being a considerate person would turn into such a great opportunity. This isn't the reason why you should treat others with respect, but it sure is a nice benefit! More importantly, I got to go about my day still in good spirits. No matter what I did, at the end of the day, my car was going to need to be fixed. I could only control how I reacted. Choose to be positive!

> "MY ATTITUDE IS THAT IF YOU PUSH ME TOWARDS SOMETHING THAT YOU THINK IS A WEAKNESS, THEN I WILL TURN THAT PERCEIVED WEAKNESS INTO A STRENGTH."
>
> —MICHAEL JORDAN, BASKETBALL PLAYER AND LEGEND

Tough times don't build character; they reveal it! You are going to go through some hard times in your life. Whether you lose your job, a loved one dies, or you suffer from a health problem, we all go through seasons. But the power of our attitude can make or break these types of situations. Are you going to give up and fold, or push on and let your true inner strength show? By embracing the situation and taking it in stride, we can show how courageous our true colors are, and this can teach us an important lesson, open a new door of opportunity, or expose us to new people that become a part of our lives for a bigger reason than we could ever realize. Practice having a good attitude in the everyday little situations, so when life's hard times come your way, you can work your way through them and come out a better person with a new perspective.

My grandfather was a wonderful example of what a person can achieve if they choose to have a positive attitude. Grandpa, or "Captian Ed" as we all called him, was the most remarkable man I ever met. Despite being small in

stature—he was a mere 5'8" (same as me!)—he was the ultimate man's man. He grew up in Alaska and did more things in his lifetime than most people could do in ten. He made a living by being a commercial fisher- man back when it was much more challenging than it is today. They didn't have the

"CAPTAIN ED" WAS A HUNTING LEGEND!

luxury of modern navigation, hydraulics, and tracking systems like today's fishermen who are watching Direct TV and streaming WIFI on their boats! Not only was Captain Ed one of the most successful seiner's in Alaska, he was also a world-renowned hunter!

To this day, he holds all kinds of records: he shot and killed some of the biggest game in the world, often with nothing more than a bow and arrow. He knew every place to hunt, every species of every kind of animal, even how to grab a piece of grass and make a call that could attract almost anything! He used to trap bears and wolverines live and send them down to zoos in California. The most famous bow and arrow hunter to date is a man by the name of Fred Bear, and Captain Ed was his guide in Alaska and led him on world record–breaking hunts! I watched several Fred Bear interviews, and I was so proud to hear him correct the interviewer every time they called him the best hunter in the world. "The best hunter in the world is a guy by the name of Ed Bilderback in Alaska. He's a better tracker, and a better shot, too!" Hanging in my grandpa's house was a big poster of Fred Bear that he signed, "To the best hunter in the world! Sincerely, Fred Bear."

Captain Ed was a larger-than-life character, and his many adventures attracted hunting enthusiast and rock star Ted Nugent. Ted interviewed him several times to hear stories about his one-of-a-kind hunting ventures with Fred Bear and other stories of his past exploits. They developed a friendship, and Captain Ed even went to a concert where Ted Nugent screamed out his name in front of thousands of fans while shooting a flaming arrow into a target! I have so many fond memories of my time spent with Captain Ed as he recounted his many hunting stories. The number of animals he killed was truly amazing, I can't repeat the exact figures because they are family secret! He even took his boat, the fifty-foot seiner *The Valiant Maid*, from Alaska to Hawaii. In Hawaii, he hunted all kinds of wild game and become something of a legend in those parts, as well. After a number of years, he brought *The Valiant Maid* back across The Pacific Ocean and continued his fishing and hunting trips in the far north.

Unfortunately, this world said goodbye to Captain Ed on January 30, 2011. Although I did not follow in the footsteps of my grandfather as a true Alaskan outdoorsmen, I am a lot like him. I am the same size he was, with much of the same coordination and quickness he had (plus a fiery competitive streak), and fortunately for me, some of his positive attitude rubbed off on me. I've had the great blessing to meet many different people who got to spend time around Captain Ed, and one thing I can say with the highest level of confidence is that people really enjoyed being around him because he was so upbeat. Nothing was impossible with grandpa; he could fix anything and figure any situation out. There didn't seem to be anything that could faze him, and this positivity, along with his charming sense of humor, made him a joy to be around. He was a people magnet. Even in his last years, people were just drawn to him, even people who were much younger and didn't totally understand the life he had led and the significance of many of the feats he had accomplished throughout the course of his life. Captain Ed was an inspiration many, and the attitude that he carried with him on a daily basis is an example that anyone can learn from and aspire to!

Captain Ed had a real bond with his boat, *The Valiant Maid*, which he owned for over fifty years. He'd seen many adventures and countries in that boat. In his later years, he took some out-of-towners out to show them some hunting spots, fell asleep after a cup of hot cocoa, and ran it into a big rock.

"ALWAYS LOOK FOR THE GOOD, ESPECIALLY IN A BAD SITUATION, AND PIVOT ON THE POSITIVE."

—MY DAD, BOB "MAMBA" LEBEAU

The boat sunk to the bottom of the bay, but luckily they were able to jump on a small raft and row away unscathed. He had grabbed a small tote and thrown it in the raft, and as they made their way away from the wreckage and watched his boat of fifty years sinking, the boat on which he had made a lifetime of memories, he said to the others with a chuckle, "At least I was able to save this tote!" Even after losing something so precious, he still found something to laugh about and was able to keep a good perspective. Grandpa was ever the optimist. In the months and years following the incident, Captain Ed was noted for saying, "I had the *Valiant Maid* for fifty-five years . . . and I only sunk it once!"

Attitude is everything.

IN CONCLUSION

"TWO ROADS DIVERGED IN A WOOD AND I,
I TOOK THE ONE LESS TRAVELED BY,
AND THAT HAS MADE ALL THE DIFFERENCE"

—ROBERT FROST, AMERICAN POET

I've used this quote by Robert Frost before, but really sums it all up. In life, you are going to constantly be given options and different choices. You can take the path of least resistance, as many do, or you can choose the path less taken. The choice is ultimately up to you. Just remember, with every decision you make, you are choosing the type of person you want to be. I don't think any of these life lessons are new principles or stray far from common sense. In fact, I don't even claim that they are original concepts. I encourage you to seek out knowledge from the world's greatest minds, as I have. Learn from people like Tony Robbins, Jack Canfield, Napoleon Hill, Abraham Lincoln, Donald Trump, and the experts in your chosen field. The pages in this book are merely a collection of some of my thoughts, research, and observations (good and bad) from application in my own life.

I've made some good choices and created some good habits, and I have done the same thing on the complete opposite end of the spectrum. Many times the wrong decisions have caused me a lot of headaches and heartache, but they have also taught me to adapt and push myself outside of my comfort zone in order to bounce back. I struggle with many of these principles on a daily basis, but it is this constant pursuit to perform and live life at the highest level that is exciting and the most rewarding. If getting what you wanted was easy, it wouldn't be as satisfying to accomplish. Who wants everything in life just handed to them on a silver platter? I know I don't. I want to be able to look back at all the obstacles I had to overcome with a smile on my face, knowing that I didn't let any of it stop me from getting to where I wanted to be.

It is my hope that these lessons and stories from my life will inspire you to live at your highest level, chase your dreams, and embrace your failures as part of the learning process on the road to success. With each "no," you are that much closer to the "yes" that can change your life forever. I hope you learn from my mistakes and that it saves you time, money, and headaches. May you be blessed on your journey, and remember, with the right attitude, anything is possible!

APPENDIX

A

LOOKING BACK: WHAT I WOULD DO DIFFERENTLY TODAY

If I were able to go back and "do it all over again," there are some things I would do differently. I would have benefitted from learning certain skills and new ways of thinking at an early age. Seeking knowledge and helping others are two of the best ways to set yourself up to have a meaningful and fulfilling life, and I encourage everyone to strive to live this way. Be like a sponge: always trying to absorb all the knowledge around that you can. Then use that knowledge to benefit not just yourself, but as many people as you can. Okay, I'll step down from my soapbox now. The following are thoughts, ideas, and suggestions I recommend to people who want to be well equipped to be successful in life.

STAND UP FOR WHAT YOU BELIEVE AND WHAT'S RIGHT

Be a leader and stand up for what you know is right. As the saying goes, "Evil flourishes when good men do nothing." Without a doubt, you are going to be in situations where you have the opportunity to stand up and say something, or back down and give in. Whether it's peer pressure, bullying, cheating on a test, stealing, or anything else, stand up for what is right! Of course, know when to pick your battles and be smart, but I can promise you that you will always be better off taking the high road.

I wish I could say I've always done this, but that is not the case. Thanks to the counsel of my family, I have, however, taken the high road a number of times when it was the last thing I wanted to do. It was so difficult! Given time to reflect on these situations, I am so thankful I took the high road. For starters, my actions showed me to be a person of good character, and people respect that. Secondly, by standing up to people who tried to treat others (or me) with disrespect, I showed them how the worth of every person. Stand up for others, and stand up for yourself. Your response to the way others talk and act towards you dictates how people will treat you in the future. Do you let people talk down to you in a disrespectful manner? Successful people don't.

I've battled with coaches, bosses, and others along the way, and I can say from experience that you will respect yourself more when you stand up for yourself. I missed out on a senior college season of basketball and lots of money from employers, which, in the short term, was a bummer, but by staying true to myself and standing up for what I knew was right, it has opened up doors and introduced me to people that have led me down a path that was so much better than I could have ever imagined. Treat others with the utmost respect, and demand the same in return. Don't ever let someone treat you like garbage, no matter if they are older, richer, or more successful. There is no one out there in the entire world that is just like you, and that in itself makes you special and valuable.

It's not always easy to stand up for what you believe, but you'll never regret it. Live a great life and find satisfaction in that. Don't be a doormat and let people walk all over you; carry yourself like the amazing person you are and demand respect from others.

Being a leader will make all the difference in your life. Unfortunately, most of the people who want to lead will take you down the wrong path. Anybody can do drugs, drink, and party. That takes no guts. Anybody can tear down weaker more vulnerable people. How hard is that to do? It actually takes some guts to be able to stand up and say "No. I'm going to be different and stand up for what I believe is right." It takes some guts to stand out among the rest and not care what other people have to say or think about you. I've found that once people find out what you believe and won't do, they actually respect you a lot more for it. That's what being a leader is to me. If you see someone bullying someone else, it is your responsibility to stand up for the weak person and say something. Speak up for the people who are too weak to speak for themselves. See the "invisible" people at your school who nobody pays any attention to. Invite them to eat lunch at your table, and take an interest in their lives. My mom instilled this in me as a kid, and I know a lot of my classmates had a better experience at school because I was willing to be their friend.

I was prime bully meat growing up. I was way smaller than everyone else, and yet I never remember getting bullied one time. I do remember one incident in the seventh grade that I think is a good example of how to handle a bully. I was in the gym shooting around during one of our breaks, and being a shorty, this wasn't always the most fun time because you'd have to wait to get a rebound, and that was a lot easier for the tall kids. I was waiting for a while beneath the basket. and finally. a shot flew in my direction and I jumped to grab it when a big eighth grader, who went by "Stormin' Norman," came out of nowhere and snatched the ball from right above me. I don't think he even jumped. He held the ball over my head, laughed at me, and I'll never forget what he said next. "What do you want to be when you grow up? A pony rider?" Apparently I wasn't even going to be big enough to even be a horse jockey (a career known for its tiny-sized people) when I grew up. It was a pretty mean thing to say; that's probably why I never forgot it. But in that moment, I had a few options of how to react: (1) I could retaliate and start a fight, which probably wasn't the best choice for a lot of reasons, but especially because he was so much bigger than me. (2) I could get upset and let him have power over me and ruin my day/week/year. Or (3) I could just ignore it not let him get any satisfaction out of my reaction, and carry on like nothing happened. I chose the last option, and Stormin' Norman never said anything to me again. I didn't let him have power over me by giving him the reaction he wanted so badly. In all honesty, I didn't care what he had to say anyway; why would I care what another person who doesn't mean anything to me has to say? I was too busy trying to get a rebound so I could shoot some three-pointers! The less you worry about what other people think and say about you, the more effective of a leader you can be. Not caring will make standing up for what you believe a lot easier.

When it comes to bullying in particular, I'd recommend you check out the work of a man I've had the great privilege to meet, Brooks Gibbs. He is the expert on the topic and is currently touring the US with the band One Direction spreading his anti-bullying message. His book *Love Is Greater Than Hate* shares his personal story with bullying growing up and lists a seven-step strategy to start a movement of kindness and compassion on your school campus. It's powerful stuff, and he is one of the top speakers on the subject in the country. I'd highly recommend watching his videos online, getting his book, and inviting him to speak to your school. Learn more about Brooks at www. BrooksGibbs.com.

GIVE BACK NOW

Giving back is transformational to your life. It will make you more grateful and appreciative of the things you are blessed to have: good family, health, a roof over your head, food to eat when you are hungry, etc. It will give you fulfillment in your life unlike any you've experienced before. You will meet and develop lasting relationships with great people who have hearts of gold and want to help others. Most importantly, you'll be making a difference in lives of others. That's what life is all about—blessing others with the blessings we've been given. Some days I just want to stay in my house and not see or talk to anybody. But that's no good. We are here to build relationships and communities, and it's something that, in all honesty, I struggle with. Try breaking out of your "me" mindset and volunteer your time, money, and efforts for those that really need it. The earlier you can take action, the better! You'll find that giving can be so rewarding, so start getting involved and volunteering NOW! You aren't getting any younger. There's tons of ways and places you can do it. Whether it's your local soup kitchen, sponsoring a needy family, or any of the organizations I've listed in Appendix C, you can make a difference. Sign up to give back somewhere today!

SOCIAL MEDIA

Social media is the biggest waste of your time and a productivity killer in the modern age. Get rid of it! Are there many wonderful things that social media allows us to do? Of course. Being able to stay in touch with friends and family and check out photos of distant relatives are all great things. But you don't need to spend all day looking at what your "friends" (let's be honest: you wouldn't even say "hi" to half the people on your friend list in real life) are saying they are doing. Everybody is their own rock star on social media. The average American spends 3 hours a day on social media. Yes, 3 hours! That's 21 hours a week and over 1,000 hours a year. That amounts to over 45 days a year spent just browsing social media. That's ridiculous! What could you do with 45 days? How about learn a new language, start a business or non-profit organization, develop a new skill or start a new hobby, volunteer to help people, create a better life for yourself and your family, make more money, or all of the above! The possibilities are endless.

Stop caring so much what your "friends" are doing or how many likes or followers you have; live life in the real world! Stop wasting your time. We have become so dang narcissistic and needy for attention and validation that we are spending all our time on social media yelling, "Look at me, look at me! I have to get a big following if I am going to be famous and successful." No, you don't. That will come when you bust your butt working hard and make the most out of the opportunities that come your way. I've got news for you: 90% of these "famous" people hire people to do all of their social media because they don't have the time or energy to tweet, post, and blog because they are too busy *actually living life*. Let's start learning from the successful people and put the phones down, shut down our computers, and start living more in the present with the people around us.

Am I saying you have to delete your Facebook, Twitter, Instagram? No. I have them. They are important in my career to build my brand. What I will not do is allow social media to waste my time and run my life. I need every minute in the day if I'm going to be successful! I also know myself, and I get too much of a kick out of how ridiculously needy for attention people are, and I can't always control my desire to make fun of them. (Hey, I never said I was perfect!) Here's the rule I live by now: 10 minutes in the morning and 10 minutes before bed for social media. That gives you plenty of time to respond to people who want to engage with you and check out a few people in your timeline.

Everything else is a waste. I wish I would had implemented this practice when I was younger! There's no telling how much more I could have accomplished if I hadn't spent half my day reading Mary Sue's obnoxious Facebook timeline. A successful person has the discipline not to waste 45 days a year and to instead put that time, energy, and brain power into the things that will make the difference between living an average life and living an extraordinary one.

TIME MANAGEMENT

Become an expert at time management. Your time is your most valuable asset. Learn to maximize every second in the day. I just showed you how to gain a 45-day-per-year edge on nearly every American. How else can you free up more time for yourself? While we are helping people along the way, we are also competing. It's just like basketball. When my hero "Pistol" Pete was asked why he worked so hard and rarely took a day off, he said "If I'm not practicing and working to get better, there might be someone else out there in another city who is practicing and getting better than me." You've got to outwork others and learn to work smarter. Start by making a daily "To–Do" list the night before. This will make your brain start subconsciously thinking about what you need to do. You'll find that you will start to have new ideas that will help you be more efficient. Your brain is constantly working, even when you are thinking about something else, so by planting those seeds in your mind the day before, you will start finding more solutions to your problems. Also, write your list in the order of what you need to do first to what you will get done last. I'd highly recommending putting your most difficult tasks first. If you knock that out at the beginning of the day, you won't be dreading it all day. You'll find that you get a lot more done once you knock out the hard stuff first because everything else will seem like a cakewalk. I implemented this strategy into my life and saw dramatic results. I think you will see the same thing if you approach your days this way.

Next, don't let people waste your time. I talked about the "friendlies" in the gym who want to talk, get in your way, and try to get you to play in pick-up games that are a waste of time. Life is full of "friendlies," people who want to waste your time, gossip, and talk your ear off about nothing. Get away from these people! As politely and kindly as possible, of course. Don't get me wrong, I am a HUGE people person. I love meeting new people, learning about them, and listening to what they do. I actually get energy and thrive off of being social, and I think it's a very important life skill to develop. Over time though, I've learned to cherish my time and not let other people waste it unnecessarily. I learned a trick from *The 4-Hour Work Week* (a book I recommend in Appendix B). Try answering the phone with the following: "Hey, I only have 2 minutes to talk before this meeting. What's up?" It may be a little white lie, but it gets people to the point and saves a lot of time that would be otherwise wasted.

Another great way to manage your time is to start saying "no" more often. Do you want to go to the movies? No. Can you help me with this project? No. Do you want to play five-on-five with us? We need one more guy! No. This can be hard at first, especially if you are like me and you are a people pleaser who doesn't want to let people down. But once you break through that initial wall and realize it's not that big of a deal and people won't get offended, you'll probably find it empowering and addictive as I have! I've found that people will respect you more for it, as well. You won't be the person who flakes because you made it seem like you were going to show up to the party when you really had no intention of attending. Are you going to the party tonight? No. I'm doing something else. It is really that easy. You can't please everybody; like Bill Cosby said: "I don't know the key to success, but the key to failure is trying to please everybody." Manage your time well, have discipline, and stay consistent.

You'll be amazed by the results.

BE THANKFUL AND HUMBLE, AND SHOW SINCERE APPRECIATION

I'm convinced that if you show others sincere appreciation and treat them with respect, you will go so much further in life. Even more importantly, it's just the right thing to do. Some of those who have exhibited these qualities to me have become my closest friends. We all want to be around good people, but we also desire to be one of those people! Be quick to praise others and thank them genuinely. Whether it's your teachers, parents, friends, the store clerk, the janitor, or whoever, a little appreciation goes a long way. Many of the people in our lives who give so much to us and others receive very little in return. I challenge you to find someone today who has gone out of their way to do something for you and just say, "Thank you." As a society, we often develop a sense of entitlement, an attitude of "the world revolves around me," and we need to work on breaking out of this mindset.

When I first moved to Hollywood, I took a commercial acting class. The funny thing is, the most valuable thing I learned in the class had nothing to do with the technique of acting! Even though the class cost me a bundle, it was worth the money I spent for just this one tip: send a hand-written thank-you note, with a $5 Starbucks card inside, to casting directors (agents, producers, etc.) who brought me in for commercial auditions . . . just to let them know I appreciated them for considering me for the job. Those little cards have been like gold for me. People lose their minds at something as small as a little appreciation. You'd think I bought them a cruise to the Bahamas by some of their reactions. It's even more meaningful to them because no one takes the time to just be grateful. This simple act will set you apart from your competition in the industry. People will remember you as a good person who was "raised right." I've also discovered that the casting directors, etc., will go above and beyond to help you after you've shown some appreciation and acknowledgement of their efforts. Try it and see for yourself. You might just find it is the best $5 you have invested in your future.

PRACTICE GETTING OUT OF YOUR COMFORT ZONE

Many times, success is just on the opposite side of fear. Your dream life can be just on the other side of that one thing that scares you the most. So your success comes down to this: are you willing to embrace your fear long enough to get your desired results?

Often, the thing we are so scared of only takes saying a few words with confidence to get on the other side of. "Would you like to go get coffee with me sometime?" "Let me get your contact information, and we can keep in touch." "I want a promotion." "I am ready to start a new career." If you let fear dictate your actions, it's going to be much harder to get your dream spouse, have your perfect job, or be truly happy. You only have to be brave for a few seconds. Usually the worst thing that happens is you get a "no." Why would you be scared of being told no? Once you start embracing fear and you get told "no" a couple times, you realize it's not really that big of a deal. In fact, it gets you that much closer to the "yes" that you want.

Jack Canfield, the author of *Chicken Soup for the Soul*, was rejected 144 times by publishers before he got a deal. He was told that readers don't like short stories, it's a stupid title, etc., etc. Well, 225 different books later, he has sold over 500 million copies in 47 languages all over the world. He's met presidents, kings, top business-men, and he is now an influential man in our modern world. He is a millionaire, and he has the ability to help new, budding authors and others worldwide for the better. What would have happened if he was scared to fail? He was rejected 144 times! Being fearless and persistent pays off.

We all know the story of Michael Jordan. He was cut from his varsity team. Yes, Michael Jordan, the greatest player of all time, wasn't good enough to make his high school team. So he threw his basketball away. Psych! We all know what really happened. His Airness took the "no" and used it to motivate himself to become the worldwide icon that he is. Don't let your fear of rejection stop you! I think MJ put it best when he said, "I've missed more than 9,000 shots in my career. I've lost almost 300 games, and 26 times I've been trusted to take the game-winning shot and missed. I've failed over and over and over again in my life, and that is why I succeed."

Even The Beatles were turned down

"ACCORDING TO MOST STUDIES, PEOPLE'S NUMBER ONE FEAR IS PUBLIC SPEAKING. NUMBER TWO IS DEATH. DEATH IS NUMBER TWO. DOES THAT SOUND RIGHT? THIS MEANS TO THE AVERAGE PERSON, IF YOU GO TO A FUNERAL, YOU'RE BETTER OFF IN THE CASKET THAN DOING THE EULOGY."

—JERRY SEINFELD, AMERICAN COMEDIAN AND ACTOR

by many record labels before they struck it big! The list goes on and on.

If you do a little research, you'll find that most hugely successful people failed repeatedly when they first started their journey. They learned early on to bounce back in life, and they learned not to be afraid to fail. There are things you can start doing now—things that I don't always like doing but that I started forcing myself to do—in order to learn how to get out of your comfort zone.

Here are some of the things you need to start doing:

Go get that beautiful girl's/cute guy's number.

I HATE doing this. I've never been good at it my whole life. I can talk and charm with the best of them, but when it comes to approaching an unknown beauty of the opposite sex, I suddenly become paralyzed with fear. Since I didn't want to do this, I knew I had to. I kept telling myself it only takes a few seconds of courage and started going for it. I'd spot the most attractive lady wherever we were at, go strike a conversation, and get her number. It's not about actually pursuing a relationship or ever calling them (although there have been a few that I definitely did call); it's all about overcoming your fear with practice.

Did I get told "no" a few times? Sure! But I realized it wasn't that big of a deal, and it didn't bother me that much at all. I was actually surprised how many times I was told "yes"! Do this with your friends so that way you can hold each other accountable. Or if your friends are like mine, you can talk smack and egg each other on to go talk to different people. Practicing this can really help you a lot when it comes to not being limited by your fears.

Another way you can practice pushing yourself outside of your comfort zone is by doing public speaking.

I don't know anyone who doesn't get at least a little nervous at the thought of getting up in front of a group of people and speaking. Most people find it nerve-wracking and intimidating. But like anything else, the more you do it, the more comfortable you become. Like going and getting girls' numbers, you just have to force yourself to do it. It only takes a short amount of courage. I've found that once I get out there and start rolling, it's not bad at all, and I actually enjoy it. Schedule yourself opportunities to do public speaking, even if you don't feel prepared to do so. That's what I did when I first started speaking.

When you are under a deadline, it forces you to make the time to prepare. Otherwise, it's much easier to remain comfortable, procrastinate, and never actually go through with it. Embrace your fear, and get out there and start talking in front of people—it doesn't even matter what it's about!

Get sales experience.

It doesn't matter what you are selling, but it is critical that you learn how to sell. Life is all about selling, whether it's an idea, product, or even yourself, we are all constantly forced to sell, sell, sell. One interesting fact I've found is that the people who make the most money with the smallest amount of education and training are usually salespeople. I spent one summer doing high-pressure time share sales (talk about stretching your comfort zone), and I benefitted tremendously from the experience. I learned many valuable lessons, one being that you can't be afraid to ask for what you want. Closed mouths don't get fed.

I also learned it's okay to be told "no." The world doesn't stop spinning. It won't kill you. "No" is just "no," and life goes on.

Another great thing I learned was how to sell myself. This is something they teach salespeople. No matter what you are selling, the consumer is buying you. If you can sell yourself, you can sell anything, whether it's a cookie or a castle. (I would recommend castles; the commission is a lot better.) There are all kinds of different jobs that will require you to sell; go get one of these jobs, and acquire important selling skills. Learn how to connect with people, speak with confidence, and adjust on the fly to cater your pitch to an individual's unique situation. Network marketing is a great way to make extra side income. I have many friends who have made great income with companies like MonaVie and Amway. See what options work best for you, and get out there and start selling!

There will never a perfect time to do anything; that's just life! You will always have an excuse. "I need to save more money." "I'm still in school." "I need to focus on getting my promotion first." "It isn't the best time of year for that."

Remember this: Everything you want is outside your comfort zone. If success was easy, everybody would have it.

That's why getting outside where you feel most comfortable is a critical thing for you to do. There are certain things that scare the crap out of me, and because of that fact, I know I have to do them. Public speaking, cold calling people I want to do business with, and publishing a book all scare me to death! In each of those endeavors, I am setting myself up to be ridiculed, judged, and hated by people. But that's what I know I am supposed to do, so I have to get past that, and the rewards have been many. The good far outweighs the bad. The fulfillment I've found in my life by breaking though my fear and the doors that have been opened by taking action have been tenfold. Break through your fears and go for it; you won't regret it!

Studies have shown that successful people take action, even if they don't always know exactly what they are doing. Learn as you go! You can't make progress if you don't go for it. As one of my acting coaches likes to say, "Leap and the net will appear!"

APPENDIX

B

BOOKS I WOULD RECOMMEND

Reading good books has changed the course of my life drastically. I am constantly motivated and inspired by the different books, articles, and information I read on a daily basis. Reading good literature has served as a tremendous educational tool and exposed me to all kinds of great new ways of thinking that have allowed me to create successful and profitable opportunities for myself. Even after you are done with school, the learning never stops! If you want to stay up to date with the latest technology, business practices, dance moves, viral videos, politics, or latest trends on Instagram, you have to keep seeking knowledge. I encourage you to embrace your role as a lifelong scholar, and here are a few books that I have benefitted from tremendously and give my highest recommendation for you to read!

JUMP SHIP: TURN YOUR PASSION INTO YOUR PROFESSION

BY JOSH SHIPP

I love the work of Josh Shipp and have been influenced by him tremendously. Josh is the top youth speaker in the world, has books and a TV show, and even trains beginning speakers on how to start their careers through his Youth Speaker University. He has programs for adults and young people and makes a huge impact in the lives of people all over the world. He often jokes that he used to get in trouble at school for running his mouth, and now he gets paid for it! He serves as a perfect example of someone who took the cards he was dealt and completely owned his life while refusing to make excuses!

His no-nonsense approach really hits home with me, and he has added a great deal of value to my life. Josh has been a mentor to me, not only as a speaker, but also as a person who holds themselves with a high level of integrity. His book, *Jump Ship: Turn Your Passion into Your Profession*, is a must read and will help you break down your limiting beliefs! If you truly want to get paid to do what you love, Josh can help you achieve just that with the practical steps he outlines in this book. If you want an amazing speaker to come to your school, organization, or event, Josh is your guy.

FOR ALL THINGS JOSH SHIPP, VISIT WWW.JOSHSHIPP.COM AND FOLLOW HIM ON TWITTER @JOSHSHIPP

THE SUCCESS PRINCIPLES: HOW TO GET FROM WHERE YOU ARE TO WHERE YOU WANT TO BE

BY JACK CANFIELD

This is one of my all-time favorite books and one that I constantly re-read. It is loaded with amazing information on how to think differently and create your dream life. It shares principles that have stood the test of time, along with endless real-life stories that will inspire and teach you valuable lessons that can bring about radical changes and results in your own life. This book has been transformational in my journey, and I encourage everyone to get a copy for themselves; it is money well spent!

IF YOU WANT TO SEE AN AWESOME, SHORT VIDEO FROM JACK CANFIELD ON THIS TOPIC, CHECK OUT THIS LINK.

RICH DAD, POOR DAD

BY ROBERT KIYOSAKI

Another great read! This book will change the way you look at your money. It will give you a new perspective on how to build your own business, create wealth, and increase your overall knowledge on your finances. We spend our whole lives working to make money; this book will help you go about it the most effective way that will teach you how to get your money working for you and not the other way around.

HOW TO WIN FRIENDS AND INFLUENCE PEOPLE

DALE CARNEGIE

This book is one of the most successful self-help books ever written. It has sold over 15 million copies worldwide to date and gives you practical techniques to:

- be more likable and make new friends while increasing your popularity,

- become a better speaker,
- earn more money and win people over to your way of thinking,
- make your home life happier,
- and much, much more.

This is truly an amazing book, and I strongly urge everyone to read it. You will really benefit as a result!

THINK AND GROW RICH

NAPOLEON HILL

This is one of the most well-known self-help books of all time and is a must read. To date, it has sold over 70 million copies! The author studied the lives and practices of many people who had accumulated a great deal of wealth and put together a list of thirteen principles that can be used to help guide people to success in any number of careers. This book can literally transform you for the better no matter what your goals or chosen profession may be! Because it was written in the 1930s, you can find it online for free. Get it. Read it. Be great.

THE 4-HOUR WORK WEEK

TIM FERRIS

This book is revolutionary. The author, Tim Ferris, just may be the real-life version of the "most interesting man in the world"! This guy is one fascinating character! He is a world traveler, speaker of five languages, crazy successful entrepreneur, world-record holding tango dancer, a national champion in Chinese kickboxing, and an actor on a popular television series in Hong Kong. Ferris has been featured in *Maxim, The New York Times, National Geographic*

Traveler, Forbes, Fortune, TIME, and hundreds of other publications. He's an angel investor and advisor for Facebook, StumbleUpon, Twitter, and Uber, to name just a few companies. He's done horseback archery in Japan, gives lectures at Princeton University, been an MTV breakdancer in Taiwan, and was named by *Wired* magazine as the "Greatest Self-Promoter of 2008." Did I mention he has had three *New York Times* bestsellers?

Tim Ferriss is a beast and a modern day genius. His books are revolutionary must-reads. I really enjoy his material, especially the way he thinks outside of the box. He will show you how to smash your fears, free up time to do the things that make life worth living, and create a lifestyle of your own design. You won't regret the small investment you pay for his books.

> GET STARTED FOR FREE BY VISITING HIS BLOG
> WWW.FOURHOURWORKWEEK.COM/BLOG/

THE CHARGE

BRENDON BURCHARD

Google Brendon Burchard and start watching his videos ASAP. He is a bestselling author, top paid speaker, and "life coach" who has helped thousands achieve financial freedom and happiness in their lives. He offers so much FREE information that has directly benefitted me in a huge way. He will motivate and change the way you think. I personally enjoy his work on "high performance." He has analyzed millionaires' habits and thinking patterns, and in his book, *The Charge,* he shows you how to be the most productive, effective, and energized person you can be every day of your life. Imagine what you could accomplish if you got up each day with a fire in your belly to be the greatest version of yourself that day. That is exactly what Brendon will show you how to do. Get his book; it's an amazing read!

YOU CAN LEARN MORE ABOUT HIM AT
WWW.BRENDONBUCHARD.COM

APPENDIX

C

ORGANIZATIONS I WOULD RECOMMEND

KIWANIS

Every young person should get involved with Kiwanis. They are the home of one of the largest youth service programs in the world. Kiwanis will provide you the opportunity to meet other like-minded people (surrounding you with great people like we've talked about) and get you involved with projects that change lives. You might just find the person whose life is changed the most is your own. Start giving back and volunteering as soon as you can; it will have a profound impact on your life and also be a lot of fun. I've found that nothing is more fulfilling than helping others.

Kiwanis also has amazing clubs that really benefit young people. I'd recommend the Key Club, which is the oldest and largest service leadership organizations for teens. They perform over 12 million service hours a year, so there are plenty of ways you can give back to your community and learn valuable leadership skills along the way. You will benefit from this club, I guarantee it.

CHECK THEM OUT AT WWW.KIWANIS.ORG

DOSOMETHING.ORG

This is a great organization that is run by folks who really get young people. DoSomething.org is the #1 organization in the US for young people and social change. They provide all kinds of opportunities for people to make a difference in the world. One thing that I find really cool about them is they are very social media savvy, so getting involved can be as easy as a text, tweet, or Facebook post. They already have gotten over 2.2 million young people involved in their campaigns to make a difference in the world. They also offer tons of free info on a wide range of topics like bullying, human rights, animals, and much, much more.

GET INVOLVED BY VISITING THEIR WEBSITE WWW.DOSOMETHING. ORG AND FOLLOWING THEM ON TWITTER @DOSOMETHING.

JUNIOR ACHIEVEMENT

Get in the Junior Achievement class at your school! One of the most important areas we need to become masters of in life is how to handle our personal finances. Whether you are rich, poor, or somewhere in the middle, being able to budget your money, invest wisely, and learn to save intelligently is vital. We hear about celebrities and pro athletes going broke all the time. It doesn't matter how much money you make; if you don't understand the money game, you are in for serious trouble. Junior Achievement offers amazing programs on financial literacy. They are in over 113 countries, reach over 10 million kids each year, and have been making a huge difference in the world for almost a hundred years now. They teach the curriculum that youth should be learning in school, as well as real-life information on jobs, money, and being an entrepreneur. If you are an adult, you can volunteer to get involved with JA as well! You can make a difference in your community by going into the classroom and teaching students from the JA financial literacy handbook. I couldn't be more excited to get involved with JA, and I hope you will reap the benefits of getting involved as well!

VISIT WWW.JUNIORACHIEVEMENT.ORG TO LEARN MORE!

YMCA

Besides having a great theme song, the YMCA is a great place to get involved. Besides having great facilities to stay fit, they also promote social responsibility, giving back to the community, camps and programs that promote leadership and education, and a ton of different learning resources! In addition to all of this, I've found that people involved with the YMCA are just good people. Go to your local YMCA and see what they have to offer. It can become a great second home for you where you can stay out of trouble, play sports, have fun, and get ahead in your studies.

TO CHECK THEM OUT ONLINE, VISIT WWW.YMCA.NET

BOYS AND GIRLS CLUB

The Boys and Girls Club is another great organization that does so much to give back and help kids. They help enable young people to reach their fullest potential as productive, caring, and responsible citizens. They give hope, offer a safe place to learn and grow, and provide life-enhancing programs and character development experiences that can impact you in a major way. They really offer a ton of great stuff that goes well beyond sports, fitness, and recreation. From leadership and character programs to the arts to life and health skills training, The Boys and Girls Club has an abundance of great opportunities for young people, and I'd encourage you to take a look for yourself and see what interests you.

VISIT WWW.BGCA.ORG TO CHECK THEM OUT!

ABOUT THE AUTHOR

JESSE LEBEAU: HIS LIFE, HIS WORDS

ver the course of the last couple years, Jesse has propelled himself from a small, Alaskan fishing town to the Hollywood big screen, being seen by millions all over the world. By leveraging his love of the game of basketball and making the most of every opportunity, he has successful created a life all his own. At 5'8", he may not be an NBA player, but by tweaking his dream, he has been able to use his passion (basketball) to star in national commercials and movies, work with pro athletes and celebrities, and even give back on a regular basis as a motivational speaker for youth. His underdog story, outlined in his book, *Among the Giants*, serves as an inspiration to anyone who has ever been told they can't make their dream a reality!

Jesse was born and raised on Pennock Island, Alaska, where his mother worked as a school teacher and his father was involved in the logging industry. Jesse played basketball growing up, but no one wanted to take him seriously, and coaches told him he was too small and would never make it. Despite his critics, he believed not only in himself but also in the plan God had for him. Jesse has experienced big wins and frustrating losses, but both triumph and defeat helped him grow as a leader and a person, and helped deepen his faith.

Today, he uses his message to motivate and inspire young people around the world as a speaker and author. Combining his love of basketball, speaking, and entertaining, Jesse founded the Fab4 Takeover, which brings celebrities into schools to teach and impact students. He also released an instructional dribbling DVD titled *Dribble Like a Star.* For a free download from the DVD visit www.JesseLeBeau.com or text the word 'DVD 'to the number 58885. You can find more information, read news in the press, watch highlight video footage, and follow Jesse on a more personal level at the following websites:

www.JesseLeBeau.com
www.fab4streetball.com
www.twitter.com/jesselebeau
www.facebook.com/jesselebeau
www.instagram.com/jesselebeau

Made in the USA
Columbia, SC
17 September 2019